A Casebook for Exploring Diversity

Merrill Titles by George L. Redman

A Casebook for Exploring Diversity, Second Edition

Teaching in Today's Classrooms: Cases from Elementary School

Teaching in Today's Classrooms: Cases from Middle and Secondary School

A Casebook for Exploring Diversity

SECOND EDITION

George L. Redman
Hamline University

Upper Saddle River, New Jersey
Columbus, Ohio

Library of Congress Cataloging-in-Publication Data

Redman, George
A casebook for exploring diversity / George L. Redman.—2nd ed.
p. cm.
Includes bibliographical references.
ISBN 0-13-093809-2 (pbk.)
1. Multicultural education—United States. 2. Pluralism (Social sciences)—United States. 3. Case method. 4. Teachers—Training of—United States. I. Title.

LC1099.3 .R43 2003
370.117'0973—dc21

2001059051

Vice President and Publisher: Jeffery W. Johnston
Executive Editor: Debra A. Stollenwerk
Editorial Assistant: Mary Morrill
Production Editor: Kimberly J. Lundy
Production Coordination: Carlisle Publishers Services
Design Coordinator: Diane C. Lorenzo
Photo Coordinator: Sandy Schaefer
Cover Designer: Linda Sorrells-Smith
Cover Art: Index Stock
Production Manager: Pamela D. Bennett
Director of Marketing: Ann Castel Davis
Marketing Manager: Krista Groshong
Marketing Services Coordinator: Tyra Cooper

This book was set in Garamond Book by Carlisle Communications, Ltd., and was printed and bound by R.R. Donnelley & Sons Company. The cover was printed by Phoenix Color Corp.

Earlier edition entitled "A Casebook for Exploring Diversity in K–12 Classrooms."

Photo Credits: Hamline University, pp. 11, 29, 55, 75, 91, 105, 119, 131, 149, 161; Silver Burdett Ginn, p. 1.

Pearson Education Ltd.
Pearson Education Australia Pty. Limited
Pearson Education Singapore Pte. Ltd.
Pearson Education North Asia Ltd.
Pearson Education Canada, Ltd.
Pearson Educación de Mexico, S.A. de C.V.
Pearson Education—Japan
Pearson Education Malaysia Pte. Ltd.
Pearson Education, *Upper Saddle River, New Jersey*

10 9 8 7 6 5 4 3 2
ISBN 0-13-093809-2

PREFACE

Book Organization

A Casebook for Exploring Diversity, Second Edition, is a text supplement for use in courses on multicultural/inclusive/urban education, as well as in foundations and methods courses in which course or program goals reflect concern for cultural diversity. It is also a useful resource in professional development programs designed to stimulate reflection and action in schools in an increasingly diverse society.

It is assumed that your primary course text will introduce, provide the theoretical and/or research base for, and show relationships among basic terms and concepts such as:

prejudice	classism
stereotype	self-esteem
discrimination	sexism
oppression	ethnicity
experiential learning	gender issues
racism	culture
exceptionality	classroom climate
multicultural curriculum	power

As a text **supplement,** the cases herein can provide (1) illustrations or examples of real classroom events, (2) problems for analysis and inquiry, and/or (3) frames for developing storied knowledge of teaching. They can create in students a need to know about concepts and/or extend thinking about such concepts. The questions at the end of each case encourage the reader to think about diversity issues as well as teaching methods, student learning, child or adolescent needs, and moral aspects of teaching.

The case analysis approach in this text is consistent with the trend toward constructivism in teacher education, in which teachers are invited to become active inquirers in their work in schools, and in so doing to emphasize reflectivity, interaction, speculative thinking, contextual influence, and personal meaning making.

The stories in this collection represent real classroom situations. Their generic nature makes them relevant to teachers and prospective teachers in grades Pre-K to 12 and throughout the full range of subject matter areas. Each case contains at least one cultural diversity issue, as well as other issues related to teaching and learning.

Features

This casebook has several characteristic features.

Provides Focused Cases

First, the cases are focused. While the cases offer opportunities for analysis on more than one level and are sufficiently complex to invite multiple interpretations, they are also more focused than many cases. As a result, instructors will find that they can be used flexibly—some of the cases may fit well in a shorter time period; for longer periods, a more lengthy case or two cases might effectively engage students.

Stimulates Thinking at Various Levels

Questions for Reflection invite students to collect further data, consider alternative perspectives, share their thoughts with others, and formulate individual or group responses. *Activities for Extending Thinking* encourage students to think about cause-and-effect relationships; develop and use categories of knowledge, skills, and dispositions; and build and evaluate new paradigms and models. At all levels, students are invited to relate insights to the course text, to field experiences, to the lesson and unit planning process, and to local, state, and national standards in teacher education.

Provides Resources for Further Study

Extensive references and resources are offered as a bridge to the knowledge base. Selected readings and Internet resources related to each of 10 diversity domains are provided at the end of each part. In addition, a list of relevant general sources is provided at the end of the book.

Provides Opportunities for Students to Become Actively Involved in Case Design

This book provides the opportunity for readers to help construct the context in which they will analyze a given case. Individuals or small groups in a course or workshop can consider a given case within more than one context. Doing so serves to highlight the importance of contextual conditions that affect teaching and learning. Suggestions for adding context are provided in Appendix A. Furthermore, to encourage active involvement in their own learning, students are invited to construct a case of their own at the end of each of 10 major parts of the text.

Provides Cases Representing Interpersonal Competence and Multicultural Content

Each case in the text falls under one or both of the classifications *interpersonal competence* or *multicultural content.* As a guide for both students and instructors, Appendix C contains a matrix placing each case into the categories of interpersonal competence (cases that focus on personal skills that demonstrate cultural sensitivity) and/or multicultural content (cases that illustrate the use of multicultural curriculum in a subject matter context).

New to This Edition

- The parts have been reorganized so that the casebook begins with a section on gender, an area of diversity that tends to have more widespread personal relevance for most pre-service classes than some of the other areas. As a result of the heightened sense of personal relevance, students are more likely to be motivated and are often more successful in these, their first attempts at analysis of cases in this text.
- A new section titled *Internet Sites for Extending Thinking* has been added to each part.
- A new part on race (Part 4) has been added. New cases include *"The Knowledge Base on Diversity: An Aid for Teachers"* (Case 13), *"Hey, My Niggah! Inclusive and/or Demeaning?"* (Case 16), and *"Hey, Teach—You Trippin' on Me, but Not on the White Kids!"* (Case 17). In addition, two cases previously included in the section on ethnicity—*"Students Right an Injustice"* (Case 14) and *"I'm Glad You're Back"* (Case 15)—have been added to the new part on race.
- A new case, *"Planning for Religious Diversity: Special Needs of Muslim Students"* (Case 24) has been added to the religion section.
- In Appendix C is a matrix identifying each case as representing an instance of interpersonal competence or multicultural content, or both.
- The "Creating Additional Context" pages, previously preceding each part, now appear in Appendix A.
- Updated and expanded knowledge-base references appear not only at the end of each of the 10 parts representing an area of diversity but also in the general bibliography section at the end of the casebook.

Format

Part 1 provides an introduction to the text, with a brief discussion of the benefits of case methodology and a description of the cases in this text, as well as the process for analyzing and discussing the cases

and for pursuing follow-up activities. Parts 2 through 11 provide cases representing key areas of cultural diversity in education. Each individual case does the following:

- Begins with a brief overview (i.e., an annotation of the story)
- Provides a concise story illustrating at least one diversity issue (some cases also provide the opportunity for analysis of pedagogical issues)
- Offers *Questions for Reflection* and *Activities for Extending Thinking*

At the end of each major section, students are invited to construct a case of their own. Finally, a bibliography and a listing of selected Internet sites relate to the diversity area of that section.

Appendices

Appendix A includes guidelines for creating additional context for a given case, a table illustrating proportions of ethnic groups represented in the U.S. population, and projections of the number of students who would comprise a "typical" classroom based on those projections.

Appendix B offers a model illustrating four levels of integration of multicultural curriculum (Banks, 2001).

Appendix C provides a matrix that identifies whether each case explores either *interpersonal competence* or *multicultural content* or both.

Related Resources

Two other casebooks are available in this series: *Teaching in Today's Classrooms: Cases from Elementary School* and *Teaching in Today's Classrooms: Cases from Middle and Secondary School.* Although some of the cases in these books may describe situations similar to those in this casebook, the primary focus of the *Questions for Reflection* in those casebooks is on pedagogy, rather than on issues of diversity. In short, the same general case situation can be used in different courses as long as the focus of study remains on issues related to respective course goals.

Acknowledgments

For their ongoing love and support, not only in the writing of this casebook, but in all my efforts, I thank my family members: Shari, Ryan, and Angie. Each truly has been a blessing in my life.

In acknowledging others who contributed to the book, I begin by thanking Dr. Eugene Anderson, professor of education (retired),

University of Minnesota. His mentorship in ways of thinking about education and teacher education has been invaluable. I have valued deeply his friendship, guidance, and support over the years. His suggestions regarding the organization and overall readability of this book have been most appreciated.

For her analysis of case-study format, validity, and integrity of concepts and her multicultural sensitivity, I thank Darcia Narváez, Department of Curriculum and Instruction, University of Minnesota. Her work significantly strengthened the conceptual and theoretical aspects of the book.

I also thank the many Pre-K to 12 teachers and undergraduate and graduate students in teacher education who reviewed the cases. Their assessment of the degree of clarity and realism of each of the cases helped greatly in confirming their potential for wider use. In particular, I thank Bonnie Houseman, English as a Second Language (ESL) teacher candidate; Jon Halpern and Jeff Fink, veteran elementary teachers; Ann Mabbott, director of Second Language Teaching and Learning at Hamline; Sam Hernandez, veteran secondary teacher; and Deborah L. Harris, parent, for their valuable reviews.

I also thank Dr. Charles Bruning, professor of education (retired), close friend and mentor. His wise counsel regarding the content of this book and his positive spirit have been encouraging indeed.

Debbie Stollenwerk, executive editor, Merrill/Prentice Hall, and Lea Baranowski, project editor, Carlisle Communications, Ltd., have done a superb job in establishing a comfortable working relationship for creating and writing. I appreciate the guidance they have so generously provided.

Katina Krull, Wayne Gannaway, Pat Burt, Kate Touhey, and Julie Miller, all of Hamline University, helped in the preparation of the manuscript.

I am also grateful to the following reviewers: Beatrice S. Fennimore, Indiana University of Pennsylvania; Barbara Kacer, Western Kentucky University; Belinda Laumbach, New Mexico Highlands University; Patricia M. Ryan, Otterbein College; and Benjamin H. Welsh, Ball State University.

Last, without the encouragement and support of my colleagues at Hamline University, completion of this casebook would not have been possible. I extend sincere thanks to each of the following members of the Education Department: Colleen Bell, Jim Bonilla, Nancy Desmond, Steve Jongewaard, Therese Kiley, Lenore Kinne, Dwight Watson, Pat Werner, and Joy Wimsatt, as well as to the college faculty as a whole.

G.L.R.

References

Banks, J. A. (2001). Approaches to multicultural curriculum reform. In J. A. Banks and C. A. Banks (Eds.), *Multicultural education: Issues and perspectives* (4th ed.) (pp. 225–246). New York: John Wiley & Sons.

Redman, G. L. (1999). *Teaching in today's classrooms: Cases from elementary school.* Upper Saddle River, NJ: Merrill/Prentice Hall.

Redman, G. L. (1999). *Teaching in today's classrooms: Cases from middle and secondary school.* Upper Saddle River, NJ: Merrill/Prentice Hall.

ABOUT THE AUTHOR

George Redman taught in the public schools for 7 years, including 4 years in the Los Angeles area and 3 in an urban school in Minneapolis. He has also taught 25 years in the undergraduate teacher education program at Hamline University in St. Paul, Minnesota; has been a continuing-studies faculty member for more than 15 years; and has conducted numerous in-service professional development workshops and courses for teachers throughout the region.

Dr. Redman's primary undergraduate responsibility has been for three courses: Education and Cultural Diversity, a core course in the program; Teaching in the Secondary School, a general methods course; and Student Teaching. He has also taught courses entitled City as Classroom, Values Education, and Self and Other. He has served as chair of the department for more than 10 years. For each of the past 25 years he has supervised student teachers in urban schools in the Minneapolis/St. Paul metropolitan area.

Professor Redman is a recipient of the Association of Teacher Educators (ATE) national award for outstanding research, and he has published numerous articles in professional journals. His other books include *Teaching in Today's Classrooms: Cases from Elementary School, Teaching in Today's Classrooms: Cases from Middle and Secondary School, Building Self-Esteem in Students: A Skill and Strategy Workbook for Teachers,* and *Building Self-Esteem in Children: A Skill and Strategy Workbook for Parents.* He is co-author of *Self-Esteem for Tots to Teens.*

CONTENTS

PART 1
INTRODUCTION

Cases: What Are They?

Cases have been defined as engaging narrative stories containing events that unfold over a period of time in a specified place (Shulman, 1992). Within teacher education, such stories describe classroom or school-related events. They are stories of either real problems or hypothetical problems representing real ones and can be as short as a paragraph or as long as 50 pages. McNergney, Herbert, and Ford (1994, p. 340) assert that "good cases have possibilities for multiple levels of analysis and they are sufficiently complex to allow multiple interpretations."

The Cases in This Casebook

The cases in this collection describe events that occur in elementary, middle, and high school classrooms in urban, suburban, and rural settings. They represent dilemmas common to all classrooms, regardless of subject matter and grade level.

Each case focuses on at least one issue involving race, socioeconomic status, language, ethnicity, gender, affectional orientation, religion, disability, parent and community involvement, or technology. In addition, each contains at least one issue related to planning, classroom environment, instruction, or professional responsibilities. Thus, each case can be used to stimulate thinking about more than one issue, depending on the orientation of a given course or workshop, and on the needs and interests of participants. For example, in one of the cases, several students ask a teacher if they can focus their research project on the contributions of a famous Native American chief rather than on one of the presidents chiseled on Mount Rushmore, as originally assigned. The instructor and participants in a particular class or workshop may decide to focus exclusively on the cultural issues within this case (e.g., how some Native Americans and members of other cultural groups may view the records of certain presidents) or to also consider the pros and cons of the instructional methodology (e.g., the project-based approach used in the case, or related issues of developing a sense of community, honoring student's choices, and the like).

Multicultural Education

A definition of the term *culture* is basic to the understanding of multicultural education. Although the term can be defined in various

ways, the broad definition offered by Pusch (1979) best serves the purpose of this text:

> Culture is the sum total of ways of living, including values, beliefs, aesthetic standards, linguistic expression, patterns of thinking, behavioral norms, and styles of communication which a group of people has developed to assure its survival in a particular physical and human environment. (p. 3)

Multiculturalism, then, invites teachers to integrate into their teaching information about the many cultures in their schools, communities, and, indeed, the world. It has as its central goal the development in all students of an understanding of, and appreciation for, the human potential of persons of all backgrounds.

Carl Grant (1994, p. 4) defines multicultural education as a "philosophical concept and an educational process." As a philosophical concept, it is based on the ideals of "freedom, justice, equality, equity, and human dignity that are contained in United States documents such as the Constitution and the Declaration of Independence" (Grant, 1994, p. 4).

As an educational process, multicultural education

> informs all academic disciplines and other aspects of the curriculum. It prepares all students to work actively toward structural equality in the organizations and institutions of the United States. It helps students to develop positive self-concepts and to discover who they are, particularly in terms of their multiple group memberships. Multicultural education does this by providing knowledge about the history, culture, and contributions of the diverse groups that have shaped the history, politics, and culture of the United States. (Grant, 1994, p. 4)

It should be emphasized that multicultural content and intercultural competence should be integrated into all content areas rather than viewed as an "add-on" subject in itself.

Finally, Banks & Banks (2001, p. 20) identifies dimensions of multicultural education that can guide school reform: (1) integration of cultural content, (2) the knowledge construction process, (3) prejudice reduction, (4) an equity pedagogy, and (5) an empowering school culture and social structure.

The more that teachers examine, reflect on, and discuss these important dimensions, the more informed they will become and the more confident they will be when implementing them in classrooms and schools. The examination of cases is one effective method for stimulating such reflection.

Cases and the Knowledge Base in Teacher Education

Case-based instruction is supported by the portion of the knowledge base that asserts that teachers' knowledge (1) is situation-specific (contextual), (2) is informed and informing through interaction (interactive), and (3) involves uncertainty (is speculative) (Clark & Lampert, 1986). Cases, then, provide situation-specific circumstances that can help students connect theory with practice in a supportive, interactive environment.

Schon (1987) observed that teachers acquire the bulk of their professional knowledge through continuous action and reflection on everyday problems. Case studies provide a common point of departure for reflecting on such problems and thus help teachers create meaning from complex teaching and learning situations.

A growing research base suggests varied benefits from reflecting on everyday problems. Through the analysis of authentic cases, teachers, businesspeople, lawyers, and others are said to develop the power to reason (Sprinthall & Theis-Sprinthall, 1983), enhance their cognitive complexity (Hunt & Sullivan, 1974; Oja & Sprinthall, 1978), perceive meaningfulness (Kennedy, 1991), alter their belief structure (Peterson, Carpenter, & Fennema, 1989), think like professionals (Kleinfeld, 1992; Morine-Dershimer, 1991), and develop other capacities through reflection. Although further research on case-method teaching is needed, interest is growing in its use to encourage the development of reflective action (McNergney, Herbert, & Ford, 1994).

Some scholars think of teacher reflection in terms of critical theory. McLaren (1989) viewed knowledge as determined by the surrounding culture, context, customs, and historical era. He observed that "critical pedagogy attempts to provide teachers . . . with a better means of understanding the role that schools actually play within a race-, class-, and gender-divided society" (p. 163).

Darling-Hammond (2000, p. 170) posits that "good teachers must develop an awareness of their own perspectives and how these can be enlarged to avoid a 'communicentric bias' (Gordon, 1990), which limits their understanding of those whom they teach." (For a review of this literature, see Darling-Hammond and Snyder, 1998)

The Benefits of Case Studies

Cases, then, provide an opportunity for both prospective and in-service teachers to address real problems; to retrieve principles of teaching and learning to resolve those problems; and to construct,

share, and evaluate responses in a community of learners. More specifically, according to Merseth (1991), as cited in Cooper (1995), case methods

1. Help develop skills of critical analysis and problem solving, including skills of observing, making inferences, identifying relationships, and articulating organizing principles.
2. Encourage reflective practice and deliberate action—they require students to discuss and choose from competing interpretations advanced by one another.
3. Provide a context in which students can make decisions in complex situations when there is not an exact match between theory and practice.
4. Involve students in their own learning—active responsibility takes the place of passive acceptance that might exist in a lecture situation.
5. Encourage the development of a community of learners by/through lively and engaging discussion and collaborative teamwork.

Tips for Preparing for Case Study Discussion

The following steps are recommended in preparing for a case study discussion:

1. Read the case quickly for general understanding.
2. Consider adding cultural and educational context in which the case is set. Suggestions for doing so are offered in Appendix A (see Creating Additional Context for the Cases).
3. Reread the case, taking notes on key issues and listing questions. Examine outside resources if time permits.
4. Complete the questions at the end of the case and the Activities for Extending Thinking assigned by your instructor.
5. Suggest ideas for activities that might extend thinking about the issue(s) in the case. For example, if you are aware of a resource or a site that could be visited by classmates to expand or refine thinking about an issue, suggest it to your instructor and your classmates.

Creating Additional Context for the Cases

In Appendix A, you will find an invitation to list community, school, and classroom factors that might make a case more rich, authentic, or personally relevant. More specifically, you are invited to list factors such as characteristics of the school and community (e.g., proportion of socioeconomic, ethnic, and religious groups) and the nature

of the individuals and the classroom in the case (e.g., personal characteristics, type of curriculum). You may also find the information in Appendix A on national estimates of various ethnic groups, children in poverty, exceptionality, and affectional orientation helpful.

Limit the number of details that you add to a given case—perhaps to four or five—so that the key issues in the case are not lost. Take a few minutes to *list in writing the contextual details you will add.* To further encourage your active participation in learning, your instructor may invite you to design a case study of your own. A form with guidelines is provided at the ends of Parts 2 through 11.

How to Participate in Class Discussions

Participation in class discussions of case studies should take place in the spirit of cooperation. Whether discussion occurs in large or small groups, your learning will be maximized if everyone has an equal opportunity to share ideas about an issue in the case.

Participants should employ good listening skills, such as those described in Anderson, Redman, and Rogers (1991) and Redman (1992), including paraphrasing, empathizing, asking open questions, asking clarifying questions, and nonverbal attending. Destructive criticism, ridicule, interrupting, and other rejecting behaviors should be avoided.

Finally, it is recommended that prior to the close of the discussion, participants share insights on *changes* in particular ideas and in the *patterns* of the responses as the discussion progressed. For example, participants may initially take the view of the teacher but through discussion may come to support the student perspective (or vice versa) in a given case. Your instructor may ask you to record this in writing.

Conclusion

Be assured that the cases you are about to examine represent real problems related to the most critical components of teaching in today's elementary, middle, and high schools—components grounded in sound research and an extensive knowledge base.

Be creative as you explore issues of diversity, relate them to field experiences or teaching experiences, design cases of your own, and utilize insights thus derived as you develop lesson and unit plans. This process helps good teachers learn and grow and become even better—it is the epitome of professional development.

References

Anderson, E. M., Redman, G. L., & Rogers, C. (1991). *Self-esteem for tots to teens.* Wayzata, MN: Parenting and Teaching Publications.

Banks, J. A., & Banks, C. A. M. (2001). *Multicultural education: Issues and perspectives.* New York: John Wiley & Sons, Inc.

Clark, C., & Lampert, M. (1986). The study of teacher thinking: Implications for teacher education. *Journal of Teacher Education, 37,* 27–31.

Cooper, J. M. (1995). Teacher's Problem Solving: A casebook of award-winning cases. Boston: Allyn & Bacon.

Darling-Hammond, L. (2000, May/June). How teacher education matters. *Journal of Teaching and Teacher Education.*

Darling-Hammond, L. & Snyder, J. (1998). Authentic Assessment of Teaching in Context. In *Contextual Teaching and Learning: Preparing Teachers to Enhance Student Success in the Workplace and Beyond.* Office of Educational Research and Improvement. Washington DC.

Gordon, E. W. (1990). Coping with communicentric bias. *Educational Researcher, 19.*

Grant, C. A. (1994). Challenging the myths about multicultural education. *Multicultural Education, 2*(2), 4–9.

Hunt, D. E., & Sullivan, E. V. (1974). *Between psychology and education.* New York: Holt, Rinehart and Winston.

Kennedy, M. M. (1991). *An agenda for research on teacher learning. (Special Report).* East Lansing, MI: National Center for Research on Teacher Learning.

Kleinfeld, J. (1992). Learning to think like a teacher: The study of cases. In J. H. Schulman (Ed.), *Case methods in teacher education* (pp. 33–49). New York: Teachers College Press.

McLaren, P. (1989). *Life in schools: An introduction to critical pedagogy in the foundations of education.* White Plains, NY: Longman.

McNergney, R., Herbert, J., & Ford, R. (1993). *Anatomy of a team case competition.* Paper presented at the annual meeting of the American Educational Research Association.

McNergney, R., Herbert, J., & Ford, R. (1994). Cooperation and competition in case-based education. *Journal of Teacher Education, 45*(5).

Merseth, K. K. (1991). *The case for cases in teacher education.* Washington, DC: American Association for Higher Education and the American Association of Colleges for Teacher Education.

Morine-Dershimer, G. (1991). Learning to think like a teacher. *Teaching and Teacher Education, 7*(2), 159–168.

Oja, S., & Sprinthall, N. A. (1978). Psychological and moral development for teachers. In N. A. Sprinthall & R. L. Mosher (Eds.), *Value development as the aim of education* (pp. 117–134). Schenectady, NY: Charter Press.

Peterson, P. L., Carpenter, T., & Fennema, E. (1989). Teacher's knowledge of student's knowledge in mathematics problem solving: Correlational and case analysis. *Journal of Educational Psychology, 81,* 558–569.

Pusch, M. D. (Ed.). (1979). *Multicultural education: A cross-cultural training approach.* Yarmouth, ME: Intercultural Press.

Redman, G. L. (1992). *Building self-esteem in students: A skill and strategy workbook for teachers.* Wayzata, MN: Parenting and Teaching Publications.

Schon, D. A. (1987). *Educating the reflective practitioner.* San Francisco: Jossey-Bass.

Shulman, L. (1992). Toward a pedagogy of cases. In J. H. Shulman, *Case methods in teacher education* (p. x). New York: Teachers College Press.

Sprinthall, N. A., & Theis-Sprinthall, L. (1983). The teacher as an adult learner: A cognitive-developmental view. *National Society for the Study of Education Yearbook* (Pt. 2), 13–35.

Internet Sites for Extending Thinking

http://curry.edschool.virginia.edu/go/multicultural/pavboard/pavboard.html Links to diversity areas such as gender, religion, ethnicity, and culture, sexuality, and others.

http://www.adl.org Anti-Defamation League materials on fighting prejudice and racism.

Part 2
Gender

Case 1

Reinforcing Specifically

Students perform assigned tasks in a class activity and receive encouragement and praise from their teacher for their efforts.

It was the last week of school before the spring break. For the past two weeks, Ms. Bell's class had worked hard on a series of lab experiments focused on factors affecting the growth rate of seeds and young pea plants. The students had demonstrated pride in learning about the structure and function of seeds and in getting their seeds to grow.

On this particular Monday, as students were completing the final lab in the series, Ms. Bell circulated throughout the room, acknowledging individual contributions to the groups of four. "I want to tell you how proud I am of your work," she said to the members of one group. "Randolf and Jon, you did especially well in creating hypotheses prior to testing the effects of temperature and light. Your ideas took into account our prior learning and at the same time were creative. Mia and Amy, your work in recording the data for your group is commendable. Your records are easier to read because they are so neatly done."

To the second group, Ms. Bell said, "Rod and Chang, your predictions as to what would happen in all of the labs in this unit were right on target! You have a good grasp of the principles of plant growth. And Sonya and Angie, your help in organizing the materials for the experiments and in checking the measurements of the plants was great. Your group couldn't have gotten the correct results without you!"

Ms. Bell provided similar feedback to the remaining two groups. All of the students seemed appreciative of her comments.

About five minutes before the bell was to ring, Ms. Bell reminded the students of their responsibilities for cleanup and the storage of lab materials. "Be sure you water your plants and return them to the window," she said. The students seemed to know their responsibilities, and they moved to store their plants and clean their tables.

Questions for Reflection

1. What was effective and ineffective about Ms. Bell's interaction with students in this case?
2. Assume that the reinforcement pattern evident in these exchanges is typical of the feedback given by Ms. Bell during the term. What effect would you suspect Ms. Bell's interaction would have on the following?
   a. Her students' achievements
   b. Their feelings of pride in their work
   c. Their self-expectations for learning in science
   d. The culture for learning in the classroom
3. What, if any, issues of diversity are embedded in this case?
4. Examine local, state, and/or national standards for teacher education and identify the standards that relate to the key issues in this case.

Activity for Extending Thinking

1. Teach a lesson in an accessible school—if you are currently in a field experience or are teaching, you may want to teach your lesson in that school. Videotape the lesson and analyze the tape for patterns of teacher-student interaction. Are there individuals and/or groups of students with whom you have more or less interaction? What types of interactions do you have with various individuals and groups (e.g., interactions that stimulate higher levels of thinking)? List the interaction patterns you have identified. Be prepared to share in class.

Case 2

Fridays Are Video Days

A teacher attends to student socializing during the Friday video.

It was Friday and Ms. Hanson loaded another videotape on the Apollo space project into the videocassette recorder. It was her opinion that if the students worked hard all week, they should be rewarded with a video on Friday. In addition to serving as a reward, the videos also varied the stimulus.

Students who were not interested in a particular video had the option of working on an extra-credit project related to the current unit of study. This month the unit was on mass and volume. On this particular Friday, Jenny, Desweon, Angie, and Ann had opted to do extra credit rather than watch the tape. In fact, the same group had chosen to do extra credit for the past three weeks.

This Friday was no different from other recent Fridays in that a group of four or five boys in the back of the room had again begun to talk during the video. For some reason, they had come to equate video watching with socializing.

To curb their talking, Ms. Hanson used proximity. Taking a seat next to the group allowed her to give them her full attention. From her vantage point, she could also see the students working on extra credit. If a student raised his or her hand for help, she could motion to the student to come to her.

When Jenny and Ann raised their hands, Ms. Hanson waved for them to come to her. Jenny pointed to a problem at the end of the chapter. "I don't get number 8," she said. "Me either," added Ann. "Let's take a look," replied Ms. Hanson. "What part *do* you understand?"

As Jenny began to respond, Ms. Hanson interrupted. "Hold that thought." She leaned toward Todd and Tim and, with her finger to her lips, said, "Shhh, please, I've asked you before not to talk during the videos. Every time I have to come over here, it takes away from the time I could be helping someone." She waited until the boys quieted down.

When she turned to Jenny, she apologized. "Sorry. Where were we?" Jenny reminded her and they began again.

Later that hour, when Teresa sought help, Ms. Hanson had to attend to the disruptive boys again.

That evening, on the way home from school, Ms. Hanson wondered about the Friday arrangement. She thought of the patterns of behavior so typical of Fridays, including having to spend much of the period with the boys in the back of the room. She listed the pros: giving the student choices (to view the video or do extra credit), varying the stimulus, rewarding student work, and giving personal attention to those who need it. Maybe the Friday arrangement was satisfactory after all.

Questions for Reflection

1. Respond to Ms. Hanson's rationale for maintaining Fridays as days that students can choose to either watch an educational video or complete extra credit work. Do you agree or disagree with her rationale? Why?
2. If you would change her Friday video activity, how would you do so? Give a rationale for any changes you suggest.
3. What issues of diversity, if any, are raised in this case?
4. What moral/ethical issues, if any, are raised in this case?

Activities for Extending Thinking

1. Design a student survey that elicits pupil opinion about the use of a particular classroom activity such as the "video day" activity. What questions would you ask?
2. List two or three ideas around which you could develop cases (stories with problems) that you could use in classes you might teach. Begin by listing the key information you want students to obtain or develop, then briefly outline a story that creates in students the desire to obtain or construct that information.
3. Examine local, state, and/or national standards for teacher education and identify the standard or standards that relate to the key issues in this case.

Case 3

Developing Skills of Critical Analysis: Exposing the Myths of Films and Fairy Tales*

A teacher guides students in the exposing of myths that perpetuate stereotypes and in using writing and speaking as vehicles for change.

Ms. Christensen wanted her students to develop the tools necessary to critique every major idea in terms of the degree to which it contributes to, or distracts from, the building of a just society. To this end, each year her class embarked on a journey of analyzing cartoons, children's movies, and stories.

This year she planned to begin by reading to the class Ariel Dorfman's *The Empire's Old Clothes: What the Lone Ranger, Babar, and Other Innocent Heroes Do to Our Minds,* in which the author claims that both popular literature and children's literature perpetuate existing power structures and deny the possibility of greater equality.

Next, as the first step in dismantling old values and constructing more just ones, the class would critique cartoons and children's movies, including *Bugs Bunny, Daffy Duck, 101 Dalmations, Pocahontas, The Lion King, Dinosaurs, The Emperor's New Groove, Sleeping Beauty, Cinderella,* and *Snow White.* The class would identify roles of people of color, as well as of men and women in the films. They would look at the power relationships among the characters; listen for loaded words, such as "backward," "primitive," and "lazy"; and consider the effect of the story on the self-image of members of a diverse audience.

In the final leg of the journey, students would share their critiques with audiences beyond the classroom. Such a step would suggest to students that their efforts were of larger import and indeed might lead to changes in their school, community, or state. Some students wrote a pamphlet to distribute to parents serving on school

*Credit for the idea on which this case is based is given to Christensen, L. (1994). Unlearning the myths that bind us. In *Rethinking our classrooms,* special edition of *Rethinking schools* (pp. 8–13). Milwaukee, WI: Rethinking Schools Limited.

advisory boards, while others watched Saturday-morning cartoons and wrote a report card for each (*Popeye* received an F because of its portrayal of ethnic groups as stupid and Americans as superior, and *Teenage Mutant Ninja Turtles* received a D because of its focus on using violence to solve problems).

Ms. Christensen noted that each year most students looked deeper into the issues and understood, for example, the master-servant relationship or how the images affected the dreams and goals of viewers or readers. A few, however, shrugged their shoulders and suggested that being rich or poor is okay, or that kids just read or view fairy tales as fun and do not really internalize the values portrayed. Ms. Christensen recalled occasional statements from students such as "Just because girls see Tinker Bell or Cinderella with tiny waists doesn't mean they'll want one." She wondered, "How can I determine how many of my students hold such beliefs and how firmly they hold them? How can I assess the degree to which my students are developing the knowledge, skills, and dispositions for thinking critically?"

Questions for Reflection

1. What did you find effective about Ms. Christensen's use of literature and movies to teach values? What might you change?
2. How would you address society's perceptions of beauty and age with your students?
3. How would you respond to the questions Ms. Christensen asked at the end of the case? More specifically:
   a. How can she determine the degree to which her class believes that stereotypes in media are not harmful?
   b. How can she determine if students are improving in their ability to think critically as they participate in this unit of instruction? (Draw on your knowledge about performance assessment, authentic assessment, and portfolios in responding to this question.)
4. Is it appropriate for teachers to challenge students' traditional social and role concepts, especially those based on family and religious values? If so, at what ages and under what conditions? How can the lessons be presented to challenge student beliefs more effectively?

Activities for Extending Thinking

1. Discuss with a parent, a teacher, and an administrator his/her philosophy about teaching values, particularly values embedded in traditional fairy tales and children's literature. Discuss both the process (methods) of teaching values and the content of the values

themselves. Include the previous "Questions for Reflection" in your discussions.

2. Critique television programs and/or commercials for their underlying values. What specific messages are sent to the viewer about gender roles?
3. Discuss with students the impact of fairy tales on conceptualizations about gender in their lives and the lives of people they know. Record your insights, and be prepared to summarize your findings in class.
4. Outline a unit plan or a series of lesson plans that would promote healthy values in a class that you might teach. Relate your product to local, state, and/or national standards for teacher education.

Case 4

Dwight, What Do You Think?

After reading a story to his class, a teacher uses a variety of questioning strategies to engage students in discussion.

Mr. Beach was beginning the third week of his first year of full-time teaching at the middle school. He had enjoyed the two years that he had been a substitute teacher, and he was excited about having his own class for the first time. His fifth hour was his favorite—a class of 25 highly motivated, limited English-proficiency students.

Mr. Beach believed strongly in the need to develop a sense of community in his class. During the first week of September, he had the class learn and practice group membership skills, including good listening skills. The students had demonstrated a high level of proficiency in using the new skills, and they seemed to have begun to feel a sense of unity as a class. In both large and small groups, students were cooperative with Mr. Beach and with one another. Now, in the third week of school, the class was reading *Love You Forever* by Robert Munsch. Mr. Beach's primary goals were to (1) help students improve in reading comprehension and (2) learn to enjoy reading. He began by having students recall previously acquired knowledge.

"Class," he said, "tell me, does it appear that persons in the story often used good listening skills when they were together?"

Several students raised their hands. Mr. Beach called on Dwight, an African-American student who sat in the front row.

"No," Dwight replied.

"What makes you say 'no'?" asked Mr. Beach.

Dwight appeared to be thinking.

After a few seconds, Mr. Beach asked, "What are the good listening skills that we learned? Let's review."

Dwight replied, "Looking at the person, not staring though, not interrupting, and being able to repeat what the person said."

"Excellent!" said Mr. Beach. "Now, as far as we can determine, did the little boy who grew up to be a man use these kinds of skills?"

"Yes," replied Dwight. "Cause he was able to say 'I'll love you forever' to his mother when she got old, so he must have listened to it when he was growing up."

"Exactly," said Mr. Beach. "Now, class, why couldn't his mother finish the saying when she was old? Mary?"

Mary thought a couple of seconds and then answered, "I'm not sure."

"Dara, what do you think?" asked Mr. Beach.

"Cause she was too old," answered Dara.

"Mahmoud, what do you think about Dara's answer?"

Mahmoud responded, "Well, she was sick, too."

"Yes, and when people get sick they get weak, don't they, sometimes too weak to talk, right?" asked Mr. Beach. Looking at Mahmoud, Mr. Beach continued, "Have you known anyone who was old and sick and almost too weak to talk?"

Mahmoud proceeded to tell the class about his grandfather who had been ill for several weeks with the flu.

Several other students mentioned persons they had known who had been ill. They talked of being sad when a loved one was ill. The discussion continued to engage the students. They completely lost track of time. Mr. Beach was pleased about the students' understanding of the story, as well as their ability to connect to prior learning. Moreover, he was pleased with his ability to lead a good, lively, and productive discussion.

Questions for Reflection

1. Assess the teacher's proficiency at using discussion and questioning techniques. What, if anything, did he do well? What positive effects did each action have on students? What, if anything, did he do that you would not recommend? Specifically, how (if at all) should he change his approach?
2. List any issues of cultural diversity embedded in this case. What should teachers do to address each issue?

Activity for Extending Thinking

1. Review at least one resource in the Readings for Extending Thinking at the end of Part 1. Summarize your insights in writing.

 DESIGN YOUR OWN CASE 

Gender Equity

Design a case that explores an issue of gender in the classroom. The story can focus on a method or strategy related to a single subject matter area (e.g., English or social studies) or on a more generic method or strategy pertinent to a wider range of subject matter areas. Your issue might also relate to:

- Planning and preparation
- Classroom environment
- Instruction
- Teacher responsibilities*

In selecting a topic, reflect on recent or current field experiences, personal experiences as a student, or accounts of real classroom incidents. Include some demographic data that tell a bit about the community, school, classroom, teacher, students, and curriculum. Include at least one problem for which there is no obvious answer. Use fictitious names of persons and schools to maintain confidentiality. Your case should be approximately two pages in length (typed, double-spaced) and should include three to four Questions for Reflection, and one or two Activities for Extending Thinking. Following is a form entitled "Design Your Own Case." It outlines categories for developing your case, as well as for developing criteria for assessing responses to your Questions for Reflection and your Activities for Extending Thinking.

*The four categories are from Danielson, C. (1996). *Enhancing professional practice: A framework for teaching*. Alexandria, VA: Association for Supervision and Curriculum Development.

Design Your Own Case

Author Name(s): ______________________________

Title of Case: ______________________ **Grade Level(s):** ________

Subject Matter Area (e.g., science): ______________________

Generic Teaching Topic (e.g., planning, grading): ______________

Contextual Information:

____

Community Factors:

____

School Factors:

____

Classroom Factors:

____

Teacher Characteristics:

____

Student Characteristics:

____

Characteristics of Curriculum:

____

Story: ______________________________________

____

____

____

____

Questions for Reflection:

1. ____

____

2. ____

____

3. ____

____

Activities for Extending Thinking:

1. ____

____

2. ____

____

Criteria for assessing responses to your Questions for Reflection:

List criteria (e.g., response is clear, consistent with research or best practice, generalized to an appropriate degree—not overgeneralized, valid—based on facts in the case, relevant to an issue in the case, other).

1. ____

____

2. ____

____

Responses to Questions for Reflection:

List what you would consider to be examples of acceptable and unacceptable responses.

	Acceptable	Unacceptable
1. a.	____________	____________
b.	____________	____________
2. a.	____________	____________
b.	____________	____________

Responses to Activities for Extending Thinking:

List examples of acceptable and unacceptable responses.

1.	____________	____________
2.	____________	____________

Readings for Extending Thinking

Alarcon, N., Castro, R., Perez, E., Pesquera, B., Riddell, A. S., & Zavella, P. (Eds.). (1993). *Chicana critical issues.* Berkeley, CA: Third Woman Press.

Andersen, M. L., & Collins, P. H. (Eds.). (1995). *Race, class, and gender: An anthology* (2nd ed.). Belmont, CA: Wadsworth.

Arias, A., Jr., & Bellman, B. (1990). Computer-mediated classrooms for culturally and linguistically diverse learners. *Computers in the Schools, 7*(1-2), 227-241.

Baca Zinn, M., & Dill, B. T. (Eds.). (1994). *Women of color in U. S. society.* Philadelphia: Temple University Press.

Belenky, M. F., Clinchy, B. M., Goldberg, N. R., & Tarrule, F. M. (1986). *Women's ways of knowing: The development of self, voice, and mind.* New York: Basic Books.

Bly, R. (1990). *Iron John: A book about men.* Reading, MA: Addison-Wesley.

Boyd, H., & Allen, R. L. (Eds.). (1995). *Brotherman: The odyssey of black men in America—An anthology.* New York: Ballantine Books.

Brown, L. (1998). *Raising their voices: The politics of girls' anger.* Cambridge, MA: Harvard University Press.

Castillo-Speed, L. (Ed.). (1995). *Latina: Women's voices from the borderlands.* New York: Touchstone/Simon & Schuster.

Cunningham, M. (1999). African-American adolescent males' perceptions of their community resources and constraints: A longitudinal analysis. *Journal of Community Psychology, 27*(5), 569-588.

de la Torre, A., & Pesquera, B. M. (1993). *Building with our hands: New directions in Chicana studies.* Berkeley: University of California Press.

DuBois, E., & Ruiz, V. (Eds.). (1994). *Unequal sisters: A multicultural reader in U. S. women's history* (2nd ed.). New York: Routledge.

Eder, D., Evans, C., & Parker, S. (1995). *Schooltalk: Gender and adolescent culture.* New Brunswick, NJ: Rutgers University Press.

Fordham, S. (1996). *Blacked out: Dilemmas of race, identity and success at Capital High.* Chicago: University of Chicago Press.

Fordham, S. (1997). A low score wins: Is high self-esteem compromising Black girls' academic achievement? Paper presented at the RISE Conference Proceedings. New Brunswick, NJ: Rutgers University, October 1999.

Frankenberg, R. (1993). *White women, race matters: The social construction of whiteness.* Minneapolis: University of Minnesota Press.

Froschl, M., Sprung, B., & Mullin-Ridler, N. (1998). *Quit It!: A Teacher's Guide on Teasing and Bullying for Use with Students in Grades K-3.* New York: Equity Concepts; Wellesley, MA: Wellesley College Center for Research on Women; Washington, DC: NEA.

Garbarino, J. (1999). *Lost boys: Why our sons turn violent and how we can save them.* New York: Free Press.

Gilligan, J. (1997). *Violence: Reflections on a National Epidemic.* New York: Vintage.

Guy-Sheftall, B. (Ed.). (1995). *Words of fire: An anthology of African-American feminist thought.* New York: The New Press.

Harris, L., & Associates, Inc. (1993). *Hostile hallways: The AAUW survey on sexual harassment in America's schools.* Washington, DC: American Association of University Women.

Hine, D. C., King, W., & Reed, L. (Eds.). (1995). *We specialize in the wholly impossible: A reader in black women's history.* Brooklyn, NY: Carlson Publishing.

Katz, J. (Ed.). (1995). *Messengers of the wind: Native American women tell their life stories.* New York: Ballantine Books.

Kivel, P. (1999). *Boys will be men: Raising our sons for courage, caring, and community.* British Columbia, Canada: New Society Publishers.

Kleinfeld, J. (1999). Student performance: Males versus females. *The Public Interest, 134*(Winter), 3–20.

Kramer, S. (1988). Sex role stereotyping: How it happens and how to avoid it. In A. O'Brien Carelli (Ed.), *Sex equity in education* (pp. 5–23). Springfield, IL: Charles C. Thomas.

Li Nim-Yu, K. (1990). Writing with pen or computer? A study on ESL secondary school learners. (ERIC Document Reproduction Service No. ED 322-720).

Maher, F. A., & Tetreault, M. K. (1994). *The feminist classroom.* New York: Basic Books.

Mid-Atlantic Equity Center. (1999). *Adolescent Boys: Statistics and Trends (A Fact Sheet).* Chevy Chase, MD: Mid-Atlantic Equity Assistance Center.

National Research Council. (1996). *National science education standards.* Washington, DC: National Academy Press.

Oakes, J. (1985). *Keeping track: How schools structure inequality.* New Haven: Yale University Press.

Orenstein, P. (1994). *Schoolgirls: Young women, self-esteem, and the confidence gap.* New York: Doubleday.

Perry, E. L., Schmidtke, J. M., & Kulik, C. T. (1998). Propensity to sexually harass: An exploration of gender differences. *Sex Roles: A Journal of Research 38*(5–6), 443–460.

Pipher, M. (1994). *Reviving Ophelia: Saving the selves of adolescent girls.* New York: Ballantine.

Sadker, D. (1999). Gender equity: Still knocking at the classroom door. *Educational Leadership, 56*(7), 22–26.

Sadker, M., & Sadker, D. (1994). *Failing at fairness: How America's schools cheat girls.* New York: Scribner's.

Sadker, M., & Sadker, D. (2000). *Teachers, schools, and society.* Boston: McGraw Hill.

Sanders, J., & Rocco, S. (1994). *Bibliography on gender equity in mathematics, science and technology: Resources for classroom teachers.* New York: Center for Advanced Study in Education, CUNY Graduate Center.

Scantlebury, K., Johnson, E., Lykens, S., Bailey, B., Clements, R., Gleason, S., Lewis, R., & Letts, W. (1996, January). *Creating a cycle of equitable teaching.* Paper presented at the annual meeting of the Association for the Education of Teachers in Science, Seattle, Washington.

Titus, J. J. (1993). Gender messages in education foundations textbooks. *Journal of Teacher Education, 44* (1), 38–43.

Wellesley Center for Research on Women. (1992). *How schools shortchange girls: A study of major findings on girls and education.* Washington, DC: American Association of University Women.

INTERNET SITES FOR EXTENDING THINKING

http://www.aauw.org American Association of University Women materials on promoting gender equality.

http://www.nmwh.org History of women's suffrage.

http://www.greatwomen.org Women who have contributed to American society; teaching ideas.

http://www/nwhp.org Clearinghouse for women's history resources, programs, and events.

http://www.looksmart.com Type "men's issues" in the "Search the Web" box and click on "Search"—links to library resources, including health and sexuality, publications for men.

Part 3
Ethnicity

Case 5

Let's All Make Up the Rules for Our Classroom

Students are given the opportunity to make real decisions regarding the operation of their classroom by helping to formulate rules for behavior.

It was the first day of the new school year. After greeting his students and describing his course goals, Mr. Chu split the class into small groups. He explained to the students that since this was their classroom as well as his, they could help make the rules for conduct. He told each group to write out several rules to recommend to the class, as well as a consequence for breaking each rule. He monitored all the groups, making notes on each student's participation. After the groups completed the assignment, he collected their lists.

That evening he reviewed the lists and developed five rules that captured some aspects of each list. He stated the rules positively; for example, if a group had written "Never talk while someone else is talking," Mr. Chu wrote "Respect others," and he gave written examples, such as "Listen when others are talking." He also included the consequence of breaking each rule, such as time-outs, loss of privileges, and detention.

When he had finished compiling the class list, he recalled that a number of the students had not participated in formulating rules and consequences for the class. He had not pressed them to contribute when he monitored the groups, but he was curious why they chose not to help create the rules. He noted further that two of the students were of Russian heritage, one a male, one a female. Another two were female students from Cambodia. Mr. Chu wondered whether cultural values, such as respect for and even dependence on adult authority, might have been the reason for their lack of response. He would ask them when he had a chance.

The next day, Mr. Chu explained how he had arrived at five collective class rules and consequences. After the class agreed that the list was acceptable, Mr. Chu wrote the rules in large letters on a sign and posted it at the front of the classroom. Mr. Chu felt confident that

by having ownership in the rules, students would be more likely to follow them.

Mr. Chu reminded the students that the next 10 minutes would be devoted to silent reading. He thought to himself, "Now would be the time to have a friendly chat with each of the four students who did not help make up the class rules." He knew he needed to be clear that he was not disappointed in them, but rather that he merely was interested in understanding why they did not participate.

Questions for Reflection

1. Was Mr. Chu rightfully concerned about the international students, or was he overreacting?
2. If the students answered "I don't know" when asked why they did not participate, what would you recommend Mr. Chu do? Is it permissible for students not to participate?
3. Imagine that you are to teach a class comprised of a large number of students of a particular ethnic group. How might the ethnicity of the students affect your approach to managing student behavior?
4. Develop a plan that you could implement in your classroom, including the following:
   a. How you would involve all students in developing the rules and procedures for classroom behavior
   b. The rules and procedures that you would hope to develop (with or without student involvement)
   c. The positive consequences of honoring the rules or procedures
   d. The negative consequences of not honoring the rules or procedures
5. What rules, if any, would be nonnegotiable?
6. How would you feel when students did not follow their own rules? How would you deal with those feelings?

Activity for Extending Thinking

1. Interview a school administrator, a school counselor, and a teacher to determine their views on involving students of various ethnicities (some of whom may feel it is not their role to participate) in establishing expectations for classroom behavior. Summarize your findings in writing, and be prepared to share in class.

Case 6

Other Cultures Celebrate Thanksgiving, Too

Thanksgiving celebrations of five different cultures are compared in a small-group reading activity.

It was mid-November when Mr. Rodriguez began his lesson on "Giving Thanks in Different Lands." He read the lesson objectives from the blackboard to his class: "Today we will learn how people of the United States have celebrated 'Thanksgiving,' as well as how people of other countries give thanks."

"How many of you have ever celebrated Thanksgiving?" he asked. Nearly all of the students raised a hand. "Please take out a sheet of paper and write what you know about Thanksgiving celebrations. Your papers will not be graded. I just want to know what you already know about our topic."

After several minutes, it appeared that all had finished writing. Mr. Rodriguez collected the papers and then read a brief story, entitled "The First Thanksgiving," a traditional account of how English settlers in North America gave thanks for their good fortune. Mr. Rodriguez raised a number of questions about the historical accuracy of the account, including whether Native Americans typically would have helped in the celebration.

"Class, now that you have heard the usual story about the 'First Thanksgiving,' I would like to extend our thinking about celebrations of thanks. It turns out that Native Americans actually had such celebrations before the English arrived in this land." For the next two minutes, Mr. Rodriguez read a short story about the first fruits ceremony and the green corn ceremony of the Wampanoags of Plymouth, Massachusetts, noting the cultural significance of each celebration.

"Now," he said, "I have stories of how four other cultures gave thanks for what they considered to be important. I have assigned pairs. I will give each pair two stories of Thanksgiving celebrations of people of other lands. I would like each of you to read one story to your partner. Take your time in reading. Your goal is to understand both of the stories completely. We will discuss them when everyone is done."

Mr. Rodriguez passed out the stories. They were "First Fruits," a celebration of the African Zulu; "Mid-Autumn Festival" the holiday of many Chinese people in San Francisco's Chinatown; "Día de Gracias," celebrated by native people of Mexico (including the Olmecas, Zapotecas, Mayas, Toltecas, Mixtecas, and Haustecas); and "Sukkot, or Feast of the Tabernacles," celebrated by Jewish people.

When the students were finished reading to one another, Mr. Rodriguez asked them to share the key aspects of each celebration with the class. He recorded critical elements of each story in four columns on the board.

He then asked, "What are some similarities about how all four groups give thanks?" After listing several, he asked, "What are some differences?" Finally, as the period was drawing to a close, he asked, "What general principles have we learned about different groups of people and how they give thanks for what they have?" Again, he listed student responses on the board.

"What have we learned about broadening our perspectives or extending our understanding of the meaning of 'First' in 'First Thanksgiving'?"

"Tomorrow," he concluded, "We will talk more about how you give thanks, as well as what today's lesson might mean to you personally. Good job today! See you tomorrow."

Questions for Reflection

1. What did Mr. Rodriguez do to help students *acquire* knowledge about Thanksgiving celebrations? What is your assessment of his technique?
2. What did Mr. Rodriguez do to *extend* and *refine* their knowledge about Thanksgiving celebrations? List the lesson steps that he had students follow.
3. How would Mr. Rodriguez's method for presenting information help students learn how to think?
4. How can a lesson such as this one contribute to goals of multicultural education? Describe other kinds of lessons that can contribute to goals of multiculturalism. Give examples of each kind of lesson.
5. What aspects, if any, of the injustices against Native Americans would you include as part of this unit?

Activities for Extending Thinking

1. Conduct a simple survey of persons of various ethnicities on the pros and cons of multiculturalism. Be prepared to summarize your findings for the class.

2. Discuss with practicing teachers methods they use for engaging students intellectually with content, or as some would say, methods for getting students to "actively construct meaning." For example, *in teaching a skill,* a teacher might tell about the skill, model (demonstrate) it, have students practice the skill with guidance, and then have students practice the skill independently. *In teaching a concept,* the teacher might define the concept, give examples and nonexamples of it, have students give examples and nonexamples, and have students demonstrate how to apply the concept. Ask the teachers how, if at all, they modify their teaching strategies to accommodate the needs of students of diverse backgrounds.

Case 7

When Will I Ever Use This? Mathematics and Social Justice

A teacher designs a math lesson that not only teaches graphing but also helps raise student awareness of social issues.

Ms. McMullen had taught fifth grade for five years. She was a competent teacher. One of her favorite subjects was math. She had kept up with developments in the field, including the use of manipulatives to help students engage in concrete activities. Moreover, she could really see that students were learning the content of the subject, and she knew it would be important in their lives as students in school and beyond.

Recently, Ms. McMullen had noticed a news report of a poll on perceptions of whites and blacks about the economic conditions of blacks in the United States of America. As she began planning for her next unit on constructing and interpreting charts and graphs, she decided that by using the current data from the article, she could teach not only math (graphing), but also a lesson on race relations.

On the first day of her unit, Ms. McMullen introduced the academic objectives of the math unit, defined some key terms, and outlined the benefits of understanding the charts and graphs. She showed how to represent data in a bar graph, a line graph, and a pie chart.

She then assigned students the task of reading and summarizing the material from a recent study on racial attitudes that was conducted by a leading national newspaper, a well-known foundation, and a nationally respected university. Finally, she informed students that they should present the data in the form of a graph. They could follow any of the charts or graphs she had introduced, but they had to be able to defend their choice. She was curious to hear the rationales they would give.

In their graphs, students were to represent survey respondents in terms of race and to depict what they considered to be key findings of the survey—for example, that 68 percent of blacks surveyed said that racism is a big problem in our society today, whereas only

38 percent of whites thought so; and 46 percent of whites said that blacks on average hold jobs of equal quality to those of whites, whereas government data show that blacks on average earn 60 percent less than whites.

Ms. McMullen planned to focus first on the mathematical aspects of the lesson and then later to connect those ideas with the issues surrounding the racial-attitude aspects of the activity.

Questions for Reflection

1. Would you support Ms. McMullen's efforts to integrate the two lessons (graphing and race relations)? Why or why not?
2. Would the cultural makeup of the class—for example, all white students, or a majority of students of color—affect your answer to question 1?
3. Have you ever taught a lesson in which you connected some "traditional" subject matter, such as graphing, reading, writing, or computing, with issues of social justice? If so, describe the lesson briefly. Describe how students responded to it. If you have not taught such a lesson, speculate on how you could teach some traditional subject matter content along with issues of social justice (e.g., race relations).

Activity for Extending Thinking

1. Interview at least two practicing teachers to learn the strategies they use to integrate social justice issues with subject matter content. Be prepared to summarize your findings in class.

Case 8

Overlook the Stereotypes—It's Art

A parent characterizes a display of photos of murals from the 1930s as depicting stereotypical images of African-Americans and women.

It was parent conference night and Ms. Lotzer was saying good night to her last parent visitor when he said to her, "By the way, those large photos with the world maps on the bulletin board, did you know that they contain stereotypical images of Africans in loincloths and 'pickaninny hairstyles'? And one has 'Aunt Jemima-like' women picking cotton. They are really insulting!"

Ms. Lotzer responded, "You know, I never thought of that. Those are photos of murals that were donated to the school by the city. They're from a collection commissioned during the Depression years to employ out-of-work artists. They were thought to have artistic value. I thought they would be better for the children than blank walls, and they do accurately portray perceptions that existed in the 1930s."

"Well, that's true, but I don't think they send the right message! In fact, in addition to the ethnic stereotypes portrayed, three of them don't depict any female images at all!"

The next day, Ms. Lotzer shared her experience with the school principal. Sympathetic to the parent's concern, the principal ordered the photos covered until it was decided whether they should be permanently removed.

The following day in class, Ms. Lotzer's students asked, "Why are the photos covered?" She told them of the events of the previous day, being careful to maintain the anonymity of the parent involved. She also mentioned that the photos would remain covered until the next faculty meeting. "At that time, I will present the parent's concerns and I hope we can agree on a reasonable policy, but for now the pictures will be covered," she said.

Some of her students seemed to support the decision of the principal, while others did not agree with his decision to cover the photos. The students asked Ms. Lotzer, "What do you plan to do?"

"I'm not sure what I'll say," she replied. "It would also be helpful, though, to know what you think—both as individuals and as a class. It would be helpful to know what more parents think," she said. "Perhaps we could devise several survey questions for parents and compile the responses. Then, I can represent not only my own views, but also those of you and your parents. Are you willing to do that?" she asked.

Hearing no objection, Ms. Lotzer asked, "Who can think of a first question that we could include in our survey?"

Questions for Reflection

1. Do you agree or disagree with the principal's decision to cover the photos?
2. What principles should teachers follow in
   a. Selecting materials for display in their classrooms?
   b. Involving students and parents in decisions regarding such issues?
   c. Countering stereotypes portrayed in other forms of media, such as television, magazines, newspapers, and electronic media, such as the Internet?
3. Did Ms. Lotzer overstep her authority in surveying students and parents without authorization from the principal?
4. What kinds of displays might be culturally commendable, yet at the same time violate ethical principles (e.g., pornography)?

Activity for Extending Thinking

1. Examine the classroom bulletin boards and display areas of several classrooms to determine whether their content contributes to the establishment of a multicultural learning environment. In what ways do displayed materials perpetuate or break down cultural stereotypes?

Case 9

Presidents of Mount Rushmore: Another Perspective

Several students ask permission to focus their research project on Native American heroes rather than the Mount Rushmore presidents assigned by the teacher.

Ms. Williams was in her third year of teaching, an endeavor that she referred to as "a privilege rather than a job."

Ms. Williams believed deeply in creating and selecting learning activities for students that were based on current events. From a newspaper article on the U.S. government's intention to clean and restore the Mount Rushmore monument (at a cost of $56 million), she designed a group project in which students were to summarize the major accomplishments and admirable traits of a president honored on Mount Rushmore. Ms. Williams thought that the project would not only refine the students' research skills, but it would also give them the opportunity to learn cooperatively.

On the day that she introduced the project to the class, she gave each student a list of the presidents honored on Mount Rushmore: Washington, Jefferson, Lincoln, and Theodore Roosevelt.

After class, Mary Bearrunner and Beth Whiteman, two Native American students, asked Ms. Williams if they could do their project on a Native American chief, such as Crazy Horse. They added that while the presidents on Mount Rushmore had done some good for whites, each had a hand in what some would call racist acts against Native Americans. "For example," said Beth, "Jefferson bought land from France that actually belonged to Native American people; and he laid the groundwork for 'Manifest Destiny,' which justified taking land and other resources without regard to the rights and cultures of others. And Lincoln approved the mass execution of 38 Indians in Mankato, Minnesota."

Ms. Williams said she would need to think about it and would let them know the next day.

Questions for Reflection

1. Write the response you would give to Mary and Beth if you were their teacher.
2. To what extent would you explore with your class the alleged "racist acts" of the presidents? Explain your response.
3. To what extent would the ethnic composition of the class affect your response to question 2?
4. What effect would your response to question 2 have on the inclusivity or the sense of community of the classroom environment?
5. What other issues related to ethnicity would you want to include in your curriculum? How would you go about including these issues?
6. Is Ms. Williams teaching "heroes history"? Should she have taken a broader ("issues") approach?
7. Do young people need heroes in order to develop character, acquire values, and have hope for the future? Explain.

Activity for Extending Thinking

1. Discuss with three or four students of a variety of ethnic backgrounds how you could better integrate multiethnic content into your curriculum. List the topics and processes that they believe should be included.

Case 10

U.S. Folk Heroes

Two Latina students ask their teacher to allow them to focus their research project on folk heroes other than those on her list of traditional U.S. folk heroes.

As in previous years, Ms. Rohlfs required her students to complete a group project in which they were to summarize the major accomplishments of a "U.S. folk hero," as well as to identify the admirable traits of that person. She thought that the project would help them refine their research and writing skills, as well as provide good lessons on values and character, lessons that she believed were needed in a society of increasing crime and violence.

On the day that she introduced the project to the class, she gave each student a list of folk heroes from whom they could choose. The list included Paul Bunyan, John Henry, Davy Crockett, and Johnny Appleseed.

After class, Rita Gonzalez and Beth Vegas, two Latina students, asked Ms. Rohlfs if they could do their project on César Chávez, Calamity Jane, or another famous frontiersperson or renowned leader in U.S. history. Ms. Rohlfs said she would need to think about it and would let them know her decision the next day.

That evening Ms. Rohlfs attended the monthly parents-teachers meeting. After the scheduled topics had been discussed, Ms. Rohlfs asked the 20 parents in attendance about adjusting her curriculum to meet the needs of Rita and Beth. While several parents seemed to encourage her to allow for variance in the curriculum, the overwhelming majority argued that the original list of folk heroes consisted of persons who truly contributed to the development of the United States and who represented values that should be promoted in schools. The majority opinion was that Rita and Beth should choose from the original list.

Questions for Reflection

1. Write out the response you would have given to Rita and Beth.
2. List the strengths and weaknesses of Ms. Rohlfs' project on U.S. folk heroes.

3. List the aspects of the project that you would modify. Why would you make those adjustments (i.e., what situations would call for them)?
4. Describe any similar experiences you have had as a student, teacher's aide, or teacher.
5. Is it important to teach values or character education in schools? If so, how is it best done? Give an example of a good lesson in values or character education.

Activity for Extending Thinking

1. Discuss with a practicing teacher, parent, and student the pros and cons of (a) teaching lessons about heroes or folk heroes and (b) teaching values or character education. Inquire about what values each feels should be taught and how those values should be addressed with students of the values and character attributes identified, which are consistent with, and which may conflict with those of other ethnic groups.

Case 11

Culture and Learning Styles

A teacher responds to a student's anxiety about giving his first oral report to the class.

Mr. Bailey wanted his students to become more confident speakers. He had given his class extensive written directions on designing and presenting an oral report. The primary goals of the activity were twofold: (1) to learn and practice presentation skills and (2) to teach the class about some of the values of another cultural group. Students were to select a cultural group that was part of their own heritage.

Several days before the presentation, Qui, a shy Cambodian student, privately expressed concerns about being able to help keep the class interested during his report. Mr. Bailey reviewed several specific presentation skills on the board.

Qui: I understand what you said about hand gestures, talking louder and softer, and looking at students, but what about the kids who aren't watching?

Mr. Bailey: Continue with your movements, changes in voice, and random eye contact. Don't stare at one or two of your classmates. You may make them nervous.

Qui: What if I can't get their attention?

Mr. Bailey: I understand how you feel, Qui. I remember the first report I gave. I thought everyone was bored out of their minds. But I concentrated on my material and found a friendly face once in a while among my classmates, and I did all right. Feeling relaxed in front of many people is difficult, but with practice and a couple of smiles and nods from me, you'll be fine. I'm sure they'll find your report very interesting—I know I want to learn more about the things you and your family consider important. And the class will really love the artwork you're bringing!

Qui: I'll do my best.

Mr. Bailey: You'll feel better if you practice at home in front of a mirror tonight. Will you do that for me?

Qui: Yes.

Mr. Bailey: See you tomorrow.

Questions for Reflection

1. Was Mr. Bailey's strategy for engagement (student reports) appropriate for Qui? Why or why not?
2. What, if any, adjustments in the lesson should he have made in light of Qui's concerns?
3. What general principles do you recommend for making adjustments in lessons for ethnically diverse students—for example, what criteria would (do) you use to determine whether you should adjust your instruction?
4. What theory, research, or practical experience supports your response to question 3?

Activity for Extending Thinking

1. Discuss with practicing teachers their methods for engaging ethnically diverse students in learning, including the most successful types of (a) activities and assignments, (b) structure and pacing of lessons, (c) grouping of students, and (d) favorite kinds of instructional materials and resources. Summarize your insights in writing and be prepared to share in class.

Case 12

Respect? Let's Talk About It

A teacher tries to establish clear standards for behavior, as well as develop in students a disposition for respecting others.

It was the second week of school. Ms. Martin was frustrated with her students. Despite her efforts at establishing and posting clear rules and consequences for behavior, several of her students were still disrespectful of others.

On Monday of the third week, Ms. Martin asked the class, "What does 'respect' mean?" Patrick raised his hand and answered, "I think respect means being kind and helpful." Ms. Martin replied, "What is an example of what you mean?" Patrick then told a story of how he had helped one of his friends with an art project. Ms. Martin thanked him for his good example.

Other students raised their hands and offered examples of respecting others' feelings and beliefs. Lee, a Vietnamese student, noted that in his culture it is respectful to look down rather than into the eyes of an adult during a conversation. Barry acknowledged that in his Native American tradition, it is a sign of respect when walking past someone to walk in front of the person rather than behind as in "white" culture. He explained further that passing in front of the person allows him or her to see that you intend no harm. James, an African-American, said that confronting him clearly and directly with directions was a sign of respect in his family. Mohammad, a student from Somalia, listed several issues of concern to Muslim students, including that students who follow the Muslim tradition strictly (1) may not participate in activities related to Halloween, Christmas, Valentine's Day, or Easter because of religious and social connotations contrary to the Islamic faith, (2) must be excused from afternoon classes for 10 to 15 minutes in order to pray in a safe area, and (3) from the onset of puberty, may not sit in close proximity to students of the opposite sex and should not be assigned to group or partner activities with members of the opposite sex. For Muslims, accommodating these beliefs and practices would be a sign of respect. The class discussed these and other examples offered by the students. Examples of what it was like *not* to be respectful were also given.

Ms. Martin listened and acknowledged each student's contribution. She then shared some stories about her own friends, including times when she was hurt because someone had been disrespectful to her. Finally, she related the class discussion to established class rules and reminded students to encourage others in following those rules.

After the discussion, Ms. Martin asked her students if they would like to decorate a bulletin board using respect as the theme. They seemed to like the idea.

Questions for Reflection

1. How do you respond to Ms. Martin's discussion of respect as a way to create a positive environment for students of all ethnicition?
2. What would you have done to make Ms. Martin's discussion even more effective?
3. What topics other than "respect" might you use in discussing behavior management issues with students?
4. What interaction strategies can a teacher use to teach students to follow classroom procedures and routines?
5. Discuss possible practical classroom accommodations that you would make to the gender/religion issue suggested by Mohammad (i.e., what strategies could you employ that would demonstrate respect for the religion aspect of the issue and yet promote gender equity?).

Activities for Extending Thinking

1. Interview three teachers about strategies they use to improve teacher-student and student-student interactions.
2. Videotape a teaching episode by a teacher, an education student in a field experience, or a clinical or peer-teaching lesson that you teach. Analyze the tape to determine teacher-student and student-student interaction patterns. (See your course text or other professional resources for interaction analysis schemes.) Does the teacher in the tape tend to interact more or less, or differently, with students of different ethnic, gender, or socioeconomic groups? If so, explain.
3. Interview teachers, students, or parents of Islamic faith. Record their views of Muslim practices that might potentially conflict with traditional U.S. educational practices (e.g., heterogeneous grouping strategies).

Design Your Own Case

Ethnicity

Design a case that explores an issue of ethnicity in the classroom. The story can focus on a method or strategy related to a single subject matter area (e.g., English or social studies) or on a more generic method or strategy pertinent to a wider range of subject matter areas. Your issue might also relate to:

- Planning and preparation
- Classroom environment
- Instruction
- Teacher responsibilities*

In selecting a topic, reflect on recent or current field experiences, personal experiences as a student, or accounts of real classroom incidents. Include some demographic data that tell a bit about the community, school, classroom, teacher, students, and curriculum. Include at least one problem for which there is no obvious answer. Use fictitious names of persons and schools to maintain confidentiality.

Your case should be approximately two pages in length (typed, double-spaced) and should include three to four Questions for Reflection and one or two Activities for Extending Thinking. Following is a form entitled "Design Your Own Case." It outlines categories for developing your case as well as for developing criteria for assessing responses to your Questions for Reflection and your Activities for Extending Thinking.

*The four categories are from Danielson, C. (1996). *Enhancing professional practice: A framework for teaching.* Alexandria, VA: Association for Supervision and Curriculum Development.

Design Your Own Case

Author Name(s): ____________________

Title of Case: ____________________ **Grade Level(s):** __________

Subject Matter Area (e.g., science): ____________________

Generic Teaching Topic (e.g., planning, grading): ____________________

Contextual Information:

____

Community Factors:

____

School Factors:

____

Classroom Factors:

____

Teacher Characteristics:

____

Student Characteristics:

____

Characteristics of Curriculum:

____

Story: ____________________

____

____

____

____

Questions for Reflection:

1. ____________________

____

2. ____________________

____

3. ____________________

____

Activities for Extending Thinking:

1. ____

____

2. ____

____

Criteria for assessing responses to your Questions for Reflection:

List criteria (e.g., response is clear, consistent with research or best practice, generalized to an appropriate degree—not overgeneralized, valid—based on facts in the case, relevant to an issue in the case, other).

1. ____

____

2. ____

____

Responses to Questions for Reflection:

List what you would consider to be examples of acceptable and unacceptable responses.

	Acceptable	Unacceptable
1. a.	____________	____________
b.	____________	____________
2. a.	____________	____________
b.	____________	____________
3. a.	____________	____________
b.	____________	____________

Responses to Activities for Extending Thinking:

List examples of acceptable and unacceptable responses.

1.	____________	____________
2.	____________	____________

Readings for Extending Thinking

African-Americans

Baker, L. D. (1998). *From Savage to Negro: Anthropology and the construction of race: 1896–1954.* Berkeley: University of California.

Egerton, J. (1994). *Speak now against the day: The generation before the civil rights movement in the South.* New York: Knopf.

Frisby, C. L. (1993). One giant step backward: Myths of black cultural learning styles. *School Psychology Review, 22,* 535–557.

Igus, T. (Ed.). (1991). *Book of black heroes: Great women in the struggle.* New York: Scholastic.

Jarrett, R. L. (1995). Growing up poor: The family experience of socially mobile youth in low-income African American neighborhoods. *Journal of Adolescent Research, 10*(1), 111–135.

Magill, F. N. (Ed.). (1992). *Masterpieces of African American literature.* New York: HarperCollins.

Southern Poverty Law Center. (1989). *Free at last: A history of the civil rights movement and those who died in the struggle.* Montgomery, AL: Teaching Tolerance.

Srickland, D. S. (1994). Educating African American learners at risk: Finding a better way. *Language Arts, 71,* 328–336.

Native Americans

Brown, D. (1970). *Bury my heart at Wounded Knee: An Indian history of the American west.* New York: Henry Holt.

Deyhle, D., & LeCompte, M. (1994). Cultural differences in child development: Navajo adolescents in middle schools. *Theory Into Practice, 33,* 156–167.

Jaimes, A. (1992). *The state of Native America: Genocide, colonization, and resistance.* Boston: South End Press.

Kast, S. (1993–1994). Mobilizing and empowering Native American youth. *Children Today, 22*(2), 27–31.

Nel, J. (1994). Preventing school failure: The Native American child. *The Clearing House, 67,* 169–174.

Reyhner, J. (1994). *American Indian/Alaska Native education.* (Phi Delta Kappa Fastback 367). Bloomington, IN: Phi Delta Kappa.

Riley, P. (Ed.). (1993). *Growing up Native American: An anthology.* New York: Morrow.

Shaffer, D. D. (1993). Making Native American lessons meaningful. *Childhood Education, 69,* 201–203.

Weatherford, J. (1991). *Native roots: How the Indians enriched America.* New York: Crown.

Asian-Americans

Chan, S. (1994). *Hmong means free: Life in Laos and America.* Philadelphia: Temple University Press.

Chong, D. (1994). *The concubine's children: The story of a Chinese family living on two sides of the globe.* New York: Penguin.

Donnelly, N. D. (1994). *Changing lives of refugee Hmong women.* Seattle: University of Washington Press.

Feng, J. (1994, June). Asian-American children: What teachers should know. *ERIC Digest,* 1-2.

Hamanaki, S. (1990). *The journey: Japanese Americans, racism, and renewal.* New York: Orchard.

Hong, M. (Ed.). (1993). *Growing up Asian American.* New York: Avon.

Okihiro, G. Y. (1994). *Margins and mainstreams: Asians in American history and culture.* Seattle: University of Washington Press.

Salyer, L. E. (1995). *Laws harsh as tigers: Chinese immigrants and the shaping of modern immigration law.* Chapel Hill: University of North Carolina Press.

Siu, S. F. (1994). *Taking no chances: Profile of a Chinese-American family's support for school success.* Boston: Wheelock College.

Takaki, R. (1989). *Strangers from a different shore: A history of Asian Americans.* Boston: Little, Brown.

Trask, H. K. (1993). *From a native daughter: Colonialism & sovereignty in Hawaii.* Monroe, ME: Common Courage Press.

Yen, C. C., & Lee, S. N. (1994). Applicability of the learning style inventory in an Asian context and its predictive value. *Educational and Psychological Measurement, 54,* 541-549.

Hispanic/Latina(o)s

Augenbraum, H., & Stavans, I. (Eds.). (1993). *Growing up Latino: Memoirs and stories.* Boston: Houghton Mifflin.

Carlson, L. M. (Ed.). (1994). *Cool salsa: Bilingual poems on growing up Latino in the United States.* New York: Henry Holt.

Casteneda, D. M. (1994). A research agenda for Mexican American adolescent mental health. *Adolescence, 29,* 225-239.

Cofer, J. O. (1990). *Silent dancing: A partial remembrance of a Puerto Rican childhood.* Houston: Arte Publico Press.

Jimenez, C. M. (1994). *The Mexican American heritage* (2nd ed., rev. and expanded). Berkeley: TQS Publications.

Kanellos, N. (1994). *The Hispanic almanac: From Columbus to corporate America.* Detroit: Visible Ink Press.

Marcell, A. V. (1994). Understanding ethnicity, identity formation, and risk behavior among adolescents of Mexican descent. *Journal of School Health, 64,* 323–327.

Mendoza, J. I. (1994). On being a Mexican American. *Phi Delta Kappan, 76,* 293–295.

Muñoz, V. I. (1995). *Where something catches: Work, love, and identity in youth.* Albany: State University of New York Press.

Ethnicity

Banks, J. A. (1997). *Teaching strategies for ethnic studies* (6th ed.). Boston: Allyn & Bacon.

Banks, J. A., & Banks, C. A. M. (Eds.). (1995). *Handbook of research on multicultural education.* New York: Macmillan.

Bialystok, E., & Hakuta, K. (1994). *In other words: The science and psychology of second-language acquisition.* New York: Basic Books.

Coballes-Vega, C. (1992, January). Considerations for teaching culturally diverse children. *ERIC Digest,* 1–2.

Crawford, J. (1992). *Hold your tongue: Bilingualism and the politics of "English only."* Reading, MA: Addison-Wesley.

Delgado, R., & Stefancic, J. (1997). *Critical white studies: Looking beyond the mirror.* Philadelphia: Temple University Press.

Delpit, L. (1995). *Other people's children: Cultural conflict in the classroom.* New York: Cambridge University Press.

Hollins, E. R., King, J. E., & Hayman, W. C. (Eds.). (1994). *Teaching diverse populations: Formulating a knowledge base.* Albany: State University of New York Press.

Irvine, J. J., & York, D. E. (1995). Learning styles and culturally diverse students: A literature review. In J. A. Banks (Eds.), *The handbook of research on multicultural education* (pp. 484–497). New York: Macmillan.

Kailin, J. (1999). How white teachers perceive the problem of racism in the schools: A case study in "liberal" Lakeview. *Teachers College Record, 100,* 724–750.

Ladson-Billings, G. (1994). *The dreamkeepers: Successful teachers of African American children.* San Francisco: Jossey-Bass.

Ladson-Billings, G. (1995). Toward a theory of culturally relevant pedagogy. *American Educational Research Journal, 32,* 465–491.

Manning, M. L., & Baruth, L. G. (1991). Appreciating cultural diversity in the classroom. *Kappa Delta Pi Record, 27*(4), 104–107.

Perez, B. (1992). Cultural and linguistic democracy: A challenge for today's schools. *Curriculum Report* (NASSP), *22*(2), 1–4.

Wang, M. C., & Gordon, E. W. (Eds.). (1994). *Educational resilience in inner-city America: Challenges and prospects.* Hillsdale, NJ: Lawrence Erlbaum.

Williams, P. J. (1995). *The rooster's egg: On the persistence of prejudice.* Cambridge: Harvard University Press.

Internet Sites for Extending Thinking

http://asianweek.com News-oriented, current events; profiles Asian stars, other success stories, and analysis of Asian business trends.

http://www.Indianz.com Updated news reports on various tribes. Health issues of American Indians, and contemporary topics.

http://hanksville.org/NAresources Links to resources on history, culture, art, language, education, and native nations.

http://www.latinolink.com News, helpful resources in areas such as music and entertainment, business and finance, sports, education, and careers.

PART 4
RACE

Case 13

The Knowledge Base on Diversity: An Aid for Teachers

Recognizing the increasing number of students of diverse racial backgrounds in her school, a teacher explores the knowledge base on racial/ethnic diversity as she makes plans for the coming year.

It was August, and Ms. Johnson was beginning to think seriously about beginning another academic year. She had taught five years, all at Washington School, but had noticed a significant change over the past two years in the demographics of the student body. In fact, the proportion of students of color had increased from 12 percent five years ago to a projected 48 percent for the coming fall.

Ms. Johnson had regularly employed principles for building self-esteem in children and youth, both in her home with her own children, as well as at work with her students. The conceptual framework that she attempted to follow included five principles for building self-esteem in students (Anderson et. al., 1991):

1. Listen to and acknowledge the thoughts and feelings of students
2. Structure situations so that they will succeed
3. Give them reasonable feelings of control over aspects of their lives
4. Reinforce them for being lovable and capable
5. Model a positive view of self

Ms. Johnson was pleased with the results from applying the principles to *all* her students over the past few years, but with the increasing number of students of color in her school, she wondered to herself if she could be doing more for them—perhaps applying the principles in a slightly different way—to better meet the needs of students of color.

She scanned the table of contents of her favorite resource by Ducette et al., (1996). Diversity in Education, in Murray (Ed.), *The Teacher Educators Handbook: Building a Knowledge Base for the Preparation of Teachers,* to get a sense of current research and recommendations for practice. With respect to diversity based on race,

she outlined a number of points that seemed to relate to the self-esteem principles with which she was familiar:

1. In studying predominantly working-class Puerto Rican and African-American students, Fine (1989) found that school administrators often censored rather than facilitated the sharing of students' experiences and ideas. For example, racism was censored so as not to demoralize students, and dropping out of school could not be discussed for it might give students ideas. Conversely, others call for *listening to and acknowledging* to students and building on their life histories and microcultural experiences (Gollnick & Chinn, 1994).
2. Murrell (1995) suggests that in order to *structure for success* for students of color, we might formulate goals that focus more on experiential knowledge in a social context, particularly as it relates to problems of race, class, gender, and culture (p. 206), and Gollnick and Chinn (1994) intimate that critically analyzing oppression and power relationships will help students understand racism, classism, sexism, and bias against the physically challenged, the young, and the aged.
3. The same authors suggest engaging students in collective social action to ensure a democratic society (Gollnick & Chinn, 1994). Others suggest sublimating traditional individualistic reward systems in favor of goals for the collective advancement of the racial/ethnic community at hand (Fordham, 1988). Such rewards may more effectively *reinforce* students of color as *lovable and capable.*
4. Still others suggest that teachers need to discuss crucial decisions made in people's lives, including difficult topics such as drug use, having a baby, and dropping out of school (Aronowitz & Giroux, 1985).
5. In a study of urban working-class students, it was found that a group of white students who believed that school would not lead to success were found to be using wealthy, not-well-educated persons in the community as role models (MacLeod, 1987). Perhaps providing more appropriate (e.g., more educated, less wealthy) models would benefit such students.

In previous years of teaching, Ms. Johnson had based her curriculum and instruction on research, theory, and what some refer to as "best practice." As she reviewed her outline of accepted studies on racial/ ethnic diversity, she began to envision ways of converting theory to practice in her own classroom. It would again be exciting to try some new ideas, this time with a new and more diverse group of students.

Question for Reflection

1. How could you translate theory to practice for each of the research-based ideas previously noted? From each of the studies previously outlined, list at least one practical strategy that you could employ in your own teaching to address those findings. Identify the grade level and subject matter area for which you intend the curriculum or instructional plan.

	Objective	Activity	Assessment Strategy
a.			
b.			
c.			
d.			
e.			

Activity for Extending Thinking

1. Using each of your responses to the Question for Reflection above, design a series of lessons that might serve as an outline of a unit plan in your own subject matter area. For example, if your response to 1 above was the following,

Objective	Activity	Assessment Strategy
Students will better understand the nature, cause, and effects of racism.	Using "racism" as the central concept,the class will employ a mapping strategy to identify prior knowledge of the nature, cause, and effects of this form of bias.	No formal grading

then you would outline 8 to 10 lesson plans that would form a general, rough draft outline of a teaching unit based on the concept of racism and related ideas.

Case 14

Students Right an Injustice

Students extend and refine reading and writing skills as they engage in a "social action" activity.

Mr. Hultgren's class had been keeping a record of upcoming class events such as field trips, student report days, and quizzes on a commercial calendar. The pictures on the calendar were of children and adolescents—mostly close-ups showing facial expressions such as wonder, excitement, happiness, and awe.

On the first day of November, Mr. Hultgren turned the page of the calendar. Hector, an outgoing youth of Mexican heritage, asked his teacher, "Mr. Hultgren, how come none of the pictures on the calendar have any kids that look like me?" Other students of color chimed in, "Yeah, or me?"

Mr. Hultgren had not paid much attention to the pictures on the calendar. "You're right," he replied, looking through the rest of the pages. "There are no children of color in the remaining pictures, either. Can anyone think of anything we could do about this?"

Marty offered a suggestion, "Perhaps we can write to the people who made the calendar and ask them to put in pictures of kids like us in their next one." The class agreed.

Mr. Hultgren briefly explained about calendar publishing companies and how they could find out to whom they should write. He then designed some activities that included prewriting, editing, rewriting, spelling, grammar and usage, and business letter format. For the next week, students devised, edited, and revised a class letter to the calendar company. The letter was sent on Friday.

Five weeks later, the class received a letter from the calendar company. It said, "Thank you for making us aware of this oversight. We apologize for our mistake and we plan to add students of color to the calendar next year."

Questions for Reflection

1. What were the strengths of Mr. Hultgren's response to the calendar problem? What else would you have done if you had been in his position?

2. List the specific behaviors of Mr. Hultgren that likely
   a. Demonstrated teacher and student efficacy
   b. Created an inclusive classroom environment
   c. Enhanced learning of academic material
3. Describe any similar experiences you have had; that is, incidents in which students have taken a social-action approach to solve a real problem in the school or broader community (see Social Action Approach in the Banks' model, Appendix B).
4. How could you design an activity that would encourage pupils to discuss the Banks' model and to identify social-action issues that they could address? How could you ensure that such a discussion was developmentally appropriate?

Activity for Extending Thinking

1. Discuss with practicing teachers, students, and parents the social problems and issues that could/should be addressed in the kinds of classes you teach or will teach. For each social problem or issue listed, identify one or two activities that would encourage students to gather relevant data, examine their own values and those of others, and take thoughtful actions to help resolve the problem or issue. (See examples in Appendix B, Social Action Approach.)

Case 15

I'm Glad You're Back

A student of color returning from an absence is given fewer days to complete a project than are his classmates.

Mr. Reese, a 25-year veteran teacher, spoke with Rod, an African-American student who had been absent for three days to take part in a school-sponsored regional band competition. The absence had been excused by the principal.

"Rod," said Mr. Reese, "I'm glad you're back. I hope your trip was fun. We have an assignment that is due the day after tomorrow. It requires a four-page paper on a person of your own heritage whom you consider to be a hero."

"But, Mr. Reese," replied Rod, "I heard that you gave Bill and Mary four days to complete the assignment and you're giving me only two days. They were absent three days, too. They were on the same trip with me."

"Well, you're not only a good student, but being African-American, you shouldn't need as much time. Bill and Mary will have more Euro-American ancestors to choose from, so for them the assignment is more complicated. I'm sure you'll do fine."

Questions for Reflection

1. What were Mr. Reese's assumptions about Rod, and on what did he base those assumptions?
2. Do you agree with the two-day timeline that Mr. Reese gave Rod? Why or why not?
3. If you were the teacher, what would you have done in this situation?
4. If Rod asked you for advice on what he should do, what would you recommend?
5. Have you observed similar situations in schools? If so, please describe briefly.

Activities for Extending Thinking

1. Interview a school ombudsperson or cultural diversity advocate. Inquire about differential treatment of students of various ethnic groups. What kinds of differential treatment (if any) are fair and what types are unfair?
2. Discuss experiences with differential treatment that students of cultural backgrounds other than that of the dominant culture have had. Be prepared to summarize your insights in class.

Case 16

Hey, My Niggah! Inclusive and/or Demeaning?

A teacher considers how to respond to four male friends—three African-American and one white—who use the racial epithet "niggah" in her classroom.

Daunte, Denzel, Michael, and Ryan had been inseparable over the past year. They had first become friends through working in small groups in one of their classes and had strengthened the bond of friendship as football buddies and in just "hanging out" after school, enjoying rap music. Most of all they seemed to enjoy having fun giving and taunting one another with friendly quips designed to both show their wit and to affirm their friendship.

Daunte, Denzel, and Michael were of African-American descent; Ryan was white. Often, taunts related to the ancestry of the four friends. "Hey, my niggah" was a greeting often extended by and to the African-American friends; "Hey, my wiggah" (the abbreviation for white nigger) was a common greeting for Ryan. For classmates who knew of their close and long-lived relationship, this form of language seemed clearly inclusive and affirming, especially when used in the informal contexts of the neighborhood and the school hallways.

However, their teacher, Ms. Persons, was new to the school and had no knowledge of the friendship of the four. Her first introduction to their jiving and taunting of one another came toward the end of the morning as the class geared down to get ready for lunch. As students put their papers and books in their bags, Ms. Persons overheard what the four friends thought was a private conversation. She also was sure that several other students overheard them as they gathered to walk together:

"What it is, my niggah?" Ryan asked Denzel.

"Hey, wigger," Denzel replied.

As Daunte approached the two, Ryan smiled. "Yo, Bro. I starved—let's go eat."

Ms. Person's ears had begun to burn after the first greeting. Her first thought was that such language should never be tolerated in any classroom. At the same time, the boys did seem to be friendly toward

one another; it was obvious that the interaction was not intended to harm. Yet what about the other students who had heard the exchange. Would ignoring the exchange give permission to others in the class to use such terms?

She didn't need this challenge on the first day of class, for she knew that it could have a significant effect on the development of respect and rapport between her and the class and among the students. Knowing she had but a few short moments to respond, she wondered what, if anything, she would say.

Questions for Reflection

1. How would you approach the boys in the previous story ? What would you say (verbatim)?
2. If you thought that because the terms "niggah" and "wigger" (wiggah) were in common use in the school and hence may be used again in your classroom, and if you therefore decided it might be best to discuss the implications of the use of such terms with your class, outline the questions that you would want to ask and the points that you would want to make in the class discussion.
   a. Questions:
   b. Points to be made:
3. What rationale would you use to explain to others (your class, parents of your students, colleagues) your decision to discuss the issue in class.
4. Is it appropriate for a white student who is referred to as a "wigger" by a close friend of color to refer to his friend of color as a "niggah"? Why or why not?
5. What other racial epithets might warrant discussion with your classes? List as many such terms as you can.

Activities for Extending Thinking

1. Review current resources on deconstructing racial epithets such as "nigger." Summarize the key insights you obtain from the readings.
2. Interview two teachers in urban schools who have had encounters such as the one in the story. Summarize their opinions on the issue of responding to the student use of such terms.
3. Interview white students and students of color who have attended urban schools with diverse student populations. Ask them about their views on the use of terms that are sometimes used as

terms of inclusivity and at other times as racial epithets. Summarize your findings in writing.

4. Knowing that your students may inadvertently encounter Web sites or print materials that use racial epithets, what preventative measures, if any, would you take to mitigate against such encounters? Would you direct students to such sites in order that they might formulate ways to counter the effects of the negative messages? Why or why not?

Case 17

Hey, Teach—You Trippin' on Me, but Not on the White Kids!

A teacher is accused of racist behavior by a student in her class.

It was Friday, the sixth week of school, and the day of the big game with the rival school. Excitement was in the air. Ms. Moss's students were caught up in the spirit of the moment as they entered her room, talking and laughing with each other. Ms. Moss liked this class and was pleased about the mutual respect that existed between her and the vast majority of her students.

The bell rang. Ms. Moss and her students had discussed and followed a clear routine for beginning class. It was understood that they had four minutes to complete their conversations, take their seats, assemble their books and papers, and cease talking. Those first four minutes of free time for the students also allowed Ms. Moss to complete attendance and to sign passes for students who were tardy or absent the previous day.

"Okay, class, it's time to begin," she said.

This day, the students were not as responsive as they usually had been in the past. Their conversations trailed on. Several students had not yet taken their seats. "Marty, Willie, Desweon, please, sit down."

When students did not respond, Ms. Moss moved toward the students who seemed to be loudest and least responsive. Her intent was to use proximity—a closer and more personal presence—to get the students' attention.

She spoke more loudly to be sure she was heard. "Desweon, Willie, I asked you to please sit down. It's time to start class."

Desweon turned to Ms. Moss. "Why you be trippin' on us? You didn't say anything to those guys," pointing to three white students across the room. "You trippin' on us cause we're black!"

"I'm trippin' on you because you're the loudest and the closest. I'm on my way to say the same thing to Marty and Tom. Now you sit down, please." Ms. Moss paused just long enough for a response, and then continued toward the white students, somewhat surprised and disappointed that she had been accused of being racist.

With personal directives to the most talkative and loudest, the class began to settle down. Ms. Moss thought to herself, "What other follow-up would be appropriate? Should I talk to Desweon and Willie in the hall? Should I discuss the incident with the class? Do I need other information about the students who were involved?" She decided to think about it overnight.

That evening as she pondered the questions from the incident that day, she also wondered about other details: Could there have been some underlying negative racial attitudes that affected her response to the class? Why didn't she approach the white students first? She had always tried to be an advocate for students of traditionally oppressed groups; she even voluntarily served as chair of the text-bias review committee for the district. Perhaps even a culturally sensitive teacher could be unknowingly influenced by some underlying attitudes. She began to think about other recent reprimands for indicators of patterns.

Questions for Reflection

1. Assess Ms. Moss's behavior in class. What behaviors, if any, were appropriate. Which, if any, were inappropriate?
2. What else, if anything, would you have done at the time of the confrontation by Desweon?
3. What, if anything, would you do as a follow-up, later that day or in the following days?
4. What local, state, and/or national standards for teacher education relate to the key issues in this case?

Activities for Extending Thinking

1. Develop a prevention plan that would minimize the likelihood of being accused of being racist by a student or students.
2. In a school setting—a field experience site or arranged visit—discuss the issue (teacher accused of racism by student) with a teacher and student of color, and with a white teacher and student. Record their suggestions for avoiding and for responding to such an issue.
3. Discuss with colleagues in your teacher preparation program incidents similar to the one above. Record their recommendations for preventing and for responding to this issue.
4. With peers or professional educators, discuss how a teacher might respond if accused by a student of being sexist, or biased in terms of socioeconomic status, ethnicity, religion, language, special needs, or affectional orientation.

 DESIGN YOUR OWN CASE 

Race

Design a case that explores an issue of race in the classroom. The story can focus on a method or strategy related to a single subject matter area (e.g., English or social studies) or on a more generic method or strategy pertinent to a wider range of subject matter areas. Your issue might also relate to:

- Planning and preparation
- Classroom environment
- Instruction
- Teacher responsibilities*

In selecting a topic, reflect on recent or current field experiences, personal experiences as a student, or accounts of real classroom incidents. Include some demographic data that tell a bit about the community, school, classroom, teacher, students, and curriculum. Include at least one problem to which there is no obvious answer. Use fictitious names of persons and schools to maintain confidentiality.

Your case should be approximately two pages in length (typed, double-spaced) and should include three to four Questions for Reflection, and one or two Activities for Extending Thinking. Following is a form entitled "Design Your Own Case." It outlines categories for developing your case as well as for developing criteria for assessing responses to your Questions for Reflection and your Activities for Extending Thinking.

*The four categories are from Danielson, C. (1996). *Enhancing professional practice: A framework for teaching.* Alexandria, VA: Association for Supervision and Curriculum Development.

Design Your Own Case

Author Name(s): ______________________________

Title of Case: ______________________ **Grade Level(s):** ________

Subject Matter Area (e.g., science): ______________________

Generic Teaching Topic (e.g., planning, grading): ______________

Contextual Information:

____

Community Factors:

____

School Factors:

____

Classroom Factors:

____

Teacher Characteristics:

____

Student Characteristics:

____

Characteristics of Curriculum:

____

Story: ______________________________

____

____

____

____

Questions for Reflection:

1. ______________________________

____

2. ______________________________

____

3. ______________________________

____

Activities for Extending Thinking:

1. ____

____

2. ____

____

Criteria for assessing responses to your Questions for Reflection:

List criteria (e.g., response is clear, consistent with research or best practice, generalized to an appropriate degree—not overgeneralized, valid—based on facts in the case, relevant to an issue in the case, other).

1. ____

____

2. ____

____

Responses to Questions for Reflection:

List what you would consider to be examples of acceptable and unacceptable responses.

	Acceptable	Unacceptable
1. a.	__________	__________
b.	__________	__________
2. a.	__________	__________
b.	__________	__________
3. a.	__________	__________
b.	__________	__________

Responses to Activities for Extending Thinking:

List examples of acceptable and unacceptable responses.

1.	__________	__________
2.	__________	__________

 READINGS FOR EXTENDING THINKING 

Anderson, E. M., Redman, & G. L., Rogers, C. (1991). *Self-esteem for tots to teens.* Wayzata, MN: Parenting and Teaching Publications.

Apple, M.W. (1997). Consuming the other: Whiteness, education, and cheap french fries. In M. Fine, L. Weis, L. Powell, & L. Wang (Eds.), *Off white: Readings on race, power, and society* (pp. 121-128). New York: Routledge.

Aronowitz, S., & Giroux, H.A. (1985). *Education under siege.* Westport, CT: Bergin & Garvey.

Asante, M. K. (1991-1992). "Afrocentric curriculum." *Educational Leadership, 49*(4), 28-31.

Bock, M., Rendon, M., & Kellogg, P. (2000). *Whiteness at work: A positive diversity curriculum.* Minneapolis, MN: Sirius Communications.

Brown, D. L. (January 13, 1999). No easy lessons on race: Black parents find new ways to prepare children. *The Washington Post,* p.A-1.

Bush, L. (1996). "The N Word." *New Yorker, 72*(10), 50.

Clark, C., & O'Donnell, J. (Eds.). (1999). *Becoming and unbecoming white: Owning and disowning a racial identity.* Westport, CT: Greenwood Press.

Council of Economic Advisors. (September, 1998). Changing America: Indicators of social and economic well-being by race and Hispanic origin. Washington, DC: United States Government Printing Office.

Cushner, M., McClelland, A., & Safford, P. (1992). *Human diversity in education: An integrative approach.* New York: McGraw-Hill.

Darling-Hammond, L. (September, 1998). Unequal opportunity: Race and education. *Brookings Review,* pp. 28-32.

Delpit, L. (1995). *Other people's children: Cultural conflict in the classroom.* New York: The New Press.

Dovidio, J. F. & Gaertner, S. L. (1998). On the nature of contemporary prejudice: The causes, consequences, and challenges of aversive racism. In J. L. Eberhardt & S.T. Fiske (Eds.), *Confronting racism: The problem and the response* (pp. 3-32). Thousand Oaks, CA: Sage.

Ducette, J., Sewell, T., & Shapiro, J. (1996). Diversity in education. In F. B. Murray (Ed.), *The Teacher Educators Handbook: Building a Knowledge Base for the Preparation of Teachers* (pps. 323-380). San Francisco: Jossey-Bass Publishers.

Dunn, R., Gemake, J. Jalali, F., & Zenhausern, R. (1990). Cross-cultural differences in learning styles of elementary-age students from four ethnic backgrounds. *Journal of Multicultural Counseling and Development, 18,* 68-93.

Dupree, D., Spencer, M. B., & Bell, S. (1997). The ecology of African-American child development: Normative and non-normative outcomes. In G. Johnson-Powell, J. Yamamoto, G. E. Wyatt, & W. Arroyo (Eds.),

Transcultural child development: Psychological assessment and treatment (pp. 237–268). New York: John Wiley & Sons, Inc.

Fine, M. (1989). Silencing and nurturing voice in an improbable context: Urban adolescents in public school. In H.A. Giroux & P. McLaren (Eds.), *Critical pedagogy, the state and cultural struggle.* Albany: State University of New York Press.

Fine, M. (1991). *Framing dropouts: Notes on the politics of urban high schools.* Albany: State University of New York Press.

Fordham, S. (1988). Racelessness as a factor in black students' school success: Pragmatic strategy or pyrrhic victory. *Harvard Educational Review, 58,* 54–84.

Foster, M. (1991). "Just got to find a way": Case studies of the lives and practice of exemplary black high school teachers. In M. Foster (Ed.), *Into schools and schooling.* New York: AMS Press.

Foster, M. (1997). *Black teachers on teaching.* New York: The New Press.

Garibaldi, A. M. (1986). Sustaining black educational progress: Challenges for the 1990s. *Journal of Negro Education, 55*(3), 386–396.

Gibbs, J.T. (1988). *Young, black and male in America: An endangered species.* Dover, DE: Auburn House.

Gollnick, D. M., & Chinn, P. C. (1994). *Multicultural education in a pluralistic society.* (4th ed.) Upper Saddle River, NJ: Merrill/Prentice Hall.

Grant, C.A., and Secada, W. G. (1991). *Preparing teachers for diversity.* In W. R. Houston (Ed.), *Handbook of research on teacher education.* New York: Macmillan.

Hale-Benson, J. E. (1982). *Black children: Their roots, culture, and learning style.* Baltimore: Johns Hopkins University Press.

Harvey, K. D., & Harjo, L. D. (1994). *Indian country: A history of native people in America.* Golden, CO: North American Press.

Joe, J. R. (1994). Revaluing Native American concepts of development and education. In P. M. Greenfield & R. R. Cocking (Eds.), *Cross-cultural roots of minority child development* (pp. 107–113). Hillsdale, NJ: Lawrence Erlbaum.

Kennedy, R. (2002). *Nigger: The strange career of a troublesome word.* New York: Pantheon Books.

Kivel, P. (1996). *Uprooting racism: How white people can work for racial justice.* Philadelphia: New Society Publishers.

Levin, S. (2000). Social psychological evidence on race and racism. In M. Chang, D. Witt, J. Jones, & K. Hakuta (Eds.), *Compelling interest: Examining the evidence on racial dynamics in higher education.* Stanford, CA: Stanford University Press.

MacLeod, J. (1987). *Ain't no makin' it: Leveled aspirations in a low-income neighborhood.* Boulder, CO: Westview Press.

Montagu, A. (1997). *Race, man's most dangerous myth: The fallacy of race.* Walnut Creek, CA: Altamira Press (Original work published 1942).

Murrell, P. C. (1995). What is missing in the preparation of minority teachers? In M. Foster (Ed.), *Into schools and schooling.* New York: AMS Press.

NAACP activists upset over dictionary's definition of the word "nigger." *Jet, 91*(3), 23–24.

The NAEP 1998 reading report card: National & state highlights. (1999). Washington, DC: Office of Educational Research and Improvement, U.S. Department of Education.

Novick, M. (1995). *White lies, white power: The fight against white supremacy and reactionary violence.* Monroe, ME: Common Courage Press.

Orfield, G., & Yun, J. T. (1999). *Resegregation in American schools.* Cambridge, MA: The Civil Rights Project, Harvard University.

Phillips, M., Brooks-Gunn, J., Duncan, G. J., Klebanov, P., & Crane, J. (1998a). Family background, parenting practices, and the Black-White test score gap. In C. Jencks & M. Phillips (Eds.), *The Black-White test score gap.* Washington, DC: Brookings Institution Press.

Phillips, M., et al. (1998b). Does the Black-White test score gap widen after children enter school? In C. Jencks & M. Phillips (Eds.), *The Black-White test score gap.* Washington, DC: Brookings Institution Press.

Rasool, J. A., & Curtis, A. C. (2000). *Multicultural education in the middle and secondary classrooms: Meeting the challenge of diversity and change.* Belmont, CA: Wadsworth/Thompson Learning.

Robinson-Zañartu, C. (1996, October). Serving Native American children and families: Considering cultural variables. *Language, speech, and hearing services in schools, 27*(4), 373–384.

School superintendent in Nevada under fire for using the word "nigger." (August 28, 2000). *Jet, 98*(12), 18.

Shade, B. J. (1989). *Culture and learning style within the Afro-American community.* New York: Stone.

Solorzano, D. G. (1998). Critical race theory, race and gender microaggressions, and the experience of Chicana and Chicano students. *International Journal of Qualitative Studies in Education, 11,* 121–137.

Steele, C. M., & Aronson, J. (1995). Stereotype threat and the intellectual test performance of African Americans. *Journal of Personality and Social Psychology, 69,* 797–811.

Tate, W. F. IV (1997). Critical race theory and education: History, theory, and implications. In M. Apple (Ed.), *Review of research in education* (pp. 195–250). Washington, DC: American Educational Research Association.

Watkins, W. H., Lewis, J. H., & Chou, V. (2001). *Race and education,* Boston: Allyn & Bacon.

Watson, D. C. (Spring, 2001). Deconstructing the "N" word. *The Hamline Review.* St. Paul, MN, 51–61.

Wellman, D. (1999). Transforming received categories: Discovering cross-border identities and other subversive activities. In C. Clark & J. O'Donnell (Eds.), *Becoming and unbecoming white: Owning and disowning a racial identity* (pp. 78–91). Westport, CT: Greenwood Press.

Wing, A. K. (Ed.). (1997). *Critical race feminism: A reader.* New York: New York University Press.

Zirkel, P. A. (1999). The "N" word. *Phi Delta Kappan, 80*(9), 713–715.

INTERNET SITES FOR EXTENDING THINKING

http://curry.edschool.virginia.edu/go/multicultural/papers/shin.html Personal narrative of a teacher on color, color blindness, and education.

http://www.seditionists.org/black/bhist.html Clearinghouse for black history resources.

http://www.altavista.com Type "african american webliography" in the "Web Page Search" box and click on "Search."

Part 5
Socioeconomic Status

Case 18

A New Student and a Lesson in Geography

An experience with a new student reminds a teacher to use caution in relating socioeconomic status to outward appearance.

As are most teachers, Mr. McDonald was dedicated and creative, and he cared about his students. Teaching was his passion. Nearly all the students in his class lived in the economically deprived neighborhood in which the school was located. Only about 15 percent of the student body were of middle-class means. It was the sixth week of school when Peter, an African-American transfer student from Chicago, entered his class. Peter was dressed like the other students, with a T-shirt and worn blue jeans. Mr. McDonald welcomed Peter into the class and gave him the usual materials: a text, handouts related to the current unit, and a set of free lunch tickets for the remainder of the week.

"Any questions?" asked Mr. McDonald.

"Yeah," Peter said. "What am I supposed to do with these tickets?"

"Just give them to the woman at the cash register in the lunchroom," replied Mr. McDonald. He then began his lesson on European history. Later in the hour, when he was well into his lesson, Mr. McDonald asked, "Can anyone tell me if one could get to Europe via the North Sea?" Peter quickly shot his hand into the air with confidence. "Yes. Actually I've crossed the North Sea by boat with my family."

Doubting that Peter had ever made such a trip, Mr. McDonald replied, "You're right, Peter: It is possible to reach Europe by the North Sea." As the hour was coming to an end, Mr. McDonald reminded students of the homework for the next day. Just as the dismissal bell rang, he finished giving the assignments.

On his way out of the room, Peter asked Mr. McDonald where he should go to get a bus pass. Mr. McDonald informed Peter that he would not need one—that all the kids walked home. Peter glanced quizzically at his new teacher and then was swallowed by the stream of students.

When Mr. McDonald made his usual stop in the principal's office the next morning to get his announcements and messages, the school secretary reminded him to have Peter pick up his bus pass. Mr. McDonald admitted that he had told Peter to walk home the day before. "Five miles!?" asked the secretary. "You know he lives in Roseville [a middle-class suburb], don't you?"

Mr. McDonald admitted that he had not known that Peter's family lived in the neighboring middle-class community. "That explains Peter's puzzled look when I handed him the free lunch tickets," he thought. Mr. McDonald wondered what he would say to Peter later that day in class.

Questions for Reflection

1. What were Mr. McDonald's assumptions about Peter, and on what did he base them?
2. In your experience as a student, what assumptions have teachers made about you because of your socioeconomic status? Briefly describe one or two incidents.
3. What kind of erroneous assumptions have you observed school personnel make based on socioeconomic status?
4. What kind of background information should teachers obtain about their new students to avoid the kinds of problems in this story? Where possible, should teachers use student files to learn about them? When no background information is available, how can teachers avoid making assumptions?
5. How could you help students in your classes understand the importance of getting to know another person rather than making assumptions based on prejudgments?

Activities for Extending Thinking

1. Talk individually with at least two students of a different socioeconomic background (avoid making assumptions when selecting your students). If you plan to use students from your field-experience placement, be sure to inform your cooperating teacher of your plans. Discuss with each student his or her likes and dislikes with respect to out-of-class activities (e.g., hobbies, sports, pets), as well as in-class preferences for learning. Be prepared to share insights.
2. Review one research-based resource from the Readings for Extended Thinking at the end of this part or from another text (e.g.,

a primary course text) that would add to your knowledge about the effects of socioeconomic status on students with whom you work. Summarize key insights in writing, and be prepared to share in class.

3. Discuss with a school administrator or counselor the teaching/learning, human development, legal and/or human-relationship competencies needed by teachers who work with students of various socioeconomic backgrounds.

Case 19

Gangs and the Victims of Violence*

Students from an economically deprived neighborhood are given a writing assignment in which they express their feelings about the hurtful effects of gang activity.

Ms. Soltow knew her students well. She was fully aware that many of her students were from homes ravaged by crime and poverty. Gang activity was commonplace. Many students had one parent at home—in most cases, a mother. Many of her students had to work at home—baby-sitting, for example—to help their working parent or parents. A number of the students had lost friends or relatives to homicide.

It was week four of school, and as usual Ms. Soltow had established a healthy rapport with her students. In an attempt to address some of their emotional needs, and at the same time to provide an opportunity for them to develop their writing abilities, Ms. Soltow addressed the class: "Often in life we are hurt by others—others who don't mean to hurt us, but nevertheless do. Can anyone give an example of how someone has hurt you?"

Raymond replied, "My brother. He's been shot twice and still hangs with a gang. It hurts me when he gets injured."

Ms. Soltow could see the pain on Raymond's face; tears had come to his eyes. "That's a good example of how we can be hurt by someone who doesn't mean to hurt us. I can see why that would cause pain. Does anyone else have a story to share?" she asked so as to give Raymond time to wipe his eyes. Several other students told similar stories.

Ms. Soltow redirected her attention to the rest of the class: "I'd like each of you to take out a sheet of paper and write about how someone has hurt you even though he or she didn't mean to. Be sure you state exactly how you felt at the time and how you feel about it now. I'll come around and help those who might like some assistance. Are there any questions before we start?"

*Based on an idea portrayed in Shapiro, A. (Executive Producer) & Fleisher, C. L. (Writer, Producer, & Director), *The truth about teachers* (videotape). Available from Pyramid Film and Video, 2801 Colorado Avenue, Santa Monica, CA 90404.

The students wrote for approximately 15 minutes while Ms. Soltow circulated, encouraging them to think further about their feelings and then to express them in writing. She provided time for volunteers to share what they could about their painful experiences. Finally, she provided a list of criteria for judging the prewriting samples and allowed the remaining 15 minutes for students to evaluate their writing on the criteria distributed.

Questions for Reflection

1. Assess Ms. Soltow's strategy of having students write about how they had been hurt by someone. Was it a suitable strategy for her students, considering their backgrounds and her instructional (writing) goals? What else, if anything, could she have done? What, if anything, should she have done differently?
2. If this case was set in an economically advantaged neighborhood, would you recommend the use of Ms. Soltow's writing strategy? Why or why not?
3. What could Ms. Soltow have done to follow-up with Raymond?
4. To what degree should teachers integrate students' personal feelings and personal lives outside of school into their instructional goals, in order to promote emotional literacy in their classes?

Activities for Extending Thinking

1. Discuss with at least one teacher, one curriculum coordinator, and one parent those factors they believe should be considered when adapting instructional goals for students from lower socioeconomic backgrounds. Be prepared to summarize your findings in class.
2. Share appropriate aspects of your own socioeconomic history with your students. Doing so will help motivate students to do the same.
3. In addition to student needs and the nature of the subject matter (e.g., English), what other factors must a teacher take into account when selecting instructional goals?
4. How could you lead your class in a discussion of the role of gangs in young people's lives and how they might find alternatives to gangs? What strategies could you use to discuss neglect, loneliness, and the subsequent low self-esteem and dependence that might attract an individual to a gang?
5. In the subject matter area in which you plan to teach, design a lesson plan that would address real socioemotional needs of students. Relate the lesson plan to a local, state, or national standard for teaching.

Case 20

How Should I Grade Danielle?

A student who fails to turn in any assigned homework and contributes little to class, yet consistently gets the highest score on tests and quizzes, causes a teacher to rethink his system for assessing students.

From the first day of the fall term, Danielle, an independent Latina student, had worn black lipstick and long sweatshirts with names of hard-rock bands on the back. As a child of factory workers, Danielle had few friends but was usually cordial to those who approached her. She generally cooperated with her teacher, Mr. Edwards.

In class, Danielle rarely turned in a homework assignment. She worked by herself when she could; when "forced" to work in a small group, she would tend to hold back and let other group members do the talking and the work. She never volunteered to answer any questions in class discussions. When Mr. Edwards would call on her, her answer would always be correct, but short. Nevertheless, she regularly had the highest quiz and test scores. In fact, on occasion she would get a perfect score, even on the larger, more difficult comprehensive unit tests.

This combination of behaviors caused a problem for Mr. Edwards. Whereas his posted daily objectives usually required students to demonstrate understanding of concepts in homework assignments or small group discussions, his grading system put the vast majority of the weight on achievement as measured by tests. With this system, Danielle would easily earn an 'A' for the term. However, he wondered if Danielle's unwillingness to complete and turn in homework assignments and her reluctance to contribute to small groups and to class discussions should be factored into her grade. Certainly her behavior was not helpful in terms of modeling to other students the behaviors in which he would like them to engage, and the behaviors most of them needed in order to succeed.

To compound his problem a bit more, Mr. Edwards would always require self-evaluations at the end of each unit. Students were to assign to themselves some number of points out of 50, and to write a two-sentence rationale for the grade assigned. Mr. Edwards believed that, in general, it was most helpful to him to see how student self-evaluations

compared with the grades he was about to assign based on the scores in his grade book. Indeed, sometimes a discrepancy between the two would help him identify an error in his record keeping, perhaps a score that inadvertently he had not recorded. For the third unit of the year, Danielle had again assigned herself a grade of 'A', using her high test scores as the basis for the grade. Mr. Edwards, a second-year teacher, often took such problems to his mentor teacher, Ms. Sundquist. Ms. Sundquist was in her ninth year as a successful teacher. "I think you need to be clear in your own mind about the outcomes you want for your students," advised Ms. Sundquist. "Your criteria and standards for assessment must be congruent with your instructional goals."

"Well," replied Mr. Edwards, "is it legitimate to have as your goals such things as 'turns in homework' and 'contributes to small and large group discussions' and the like? If these are legitimate goals, then Danielle should perhaps get a 'B' or 'C'. But when she has the highest test scores in the entire grade level, I'd have a hard time justifying that to her or her parents!"

"To be fair to students," asserted Ms. Sundquist, "the goals need to be meaningful and the students need to be clear about the criteria upon which their performances will be judged. For example, if asked to write a descriptive essay, they need to know if they will be assessed on specifics, such as organization, creativity, grammar and usage, spelling, punctuation, and/or other possible criteria for assessment. Some scholars recommend identifying levels of goal attainment on each of the standards—for example, for organization: What type of response would earn a high grade, an average grade, or a low grade? The literature recommends that assessments be authentic; that is, that they reflect real-world applications whenever possible. I'll show you what I do if you'd like."

"Yes, I'd appreciate that," said Mr. Edwards. "I'd also like to explore strategies for using peer evaluations and portfolios, including electronic portfolios. I hear Mr. Boeck has a computer program for electronic portfolios."

"You have some challenging questions. Let's start with examples of how I design authentic performance assessments for my class. I'll bring some to our mentor-mentee meeting on Friday."

Questions for Reflection

1. What grade should Mr. Edwards assign to Danielle? What is your rationale for assigning that grade?
2. To what extent was your assessment influenced by Danielle's socioeconomic background? What other factors influenced your assessment?

3. What changes, if any, should Mr. Edwards make in his plan for assessing students? Why are those changes needed?
4. Might a student's social class and economic status affect his or her achievements? If so, in what ways?
5. What assessment techniques might be less fair and more fair to students of lower-income families? Why?

Activities for Extending Thinking

1. Interview at least one experienced practicing teacher to determine (a) his or her desired student outcomes for a given unit and (b) the standards and criteria for assessing those outcomes. Explore the degree to which the means of assessment are fair and supportive of students of lower-income families.
2. Interview at least one experienced practicing teacher to ascertain how, if at all, the teacher's plan for assessment and grading accommodates students of lower-income status.
3. Outline a plan to involve students in developing criteria to be used in assessing their work.

Case 21

Rewarding Respectful Behavior

A teacher uses a behavior modification plan to encourage two students to become more respectful of classmates.

Ms. Anderson was having trouble with two students in her class: Tommy, an energetic student of color from a low-income, blue-collar home, and Delia, a bright student from an upper-middle-class family. They often called their fellow students names—sometimes even using profanity—and did not seem to care about others' feelings. No matter how many times a day Ms. Anderson reprimanded them, they did not seem to change. One day she offered them a deal. For every time they were thoughtful of another student—such as when they offered to help another student, when they shared, when they said nice things without name-calling or profanity—they would receive a point. When they reached 20 points, they would be allowed to choose a reward from a predetermined list that Tommy, Delia, and Ms. Anderson made together. The point total would be displayed on a chart at Ms. Anderson's desk for them to see whenever they wished.

Tommy enjoyed the challenge and began to say "please" and "thank you" to fellow students and always asked permission before using what belonged to others. He stopped making rude comments to the other students and even played with them without incident. Ms. Anderson told Tommy she was pleased with the change in his behavior.

Delia, however, continued her disrespectful ways. Ms. Anderson considered contacting Delia's parents, but a rumor that her parents were strict and harsh led her to reconsider. She decided to ask other teachers and counselors for recommendations about handling Delia's rude behavior. Perhaps her colleagues could help.

Questions for Reflection

1. To what extent have you used an incentive/reward system such as the one Ms. Anderson used with Tommy and Delia? Under what circumstances would you use such a system?

2. Identify the strengths of such a system.
3. Identify the weaknesses of such a system.
4. How might child-rearing practices in lower-income homes affect student behavior? Should child-rearing practices affect how a teacher manages student behavior?

Activities for Extending Thinking

1. Interview parents of students of two or three different socioeconomic levels regarding the disciplinary policies and practices they prefer.
2. Read a theoretical or empirical research account of the relationship between socioeconomic status and family approaches to discipline. Be prepared to share key insights with your class.

 Design Your Own Case 

Socioeconomic Status

Design a case that explores an issue of socioeconomic status in the classroom. The story can focus on a method or strategy related to a single subject matter area (e.g., English or social studies) or on a more generic method or strategy pertinent to a wider range of subject matter areas. Your issue might also relate to:

- Planning and preparation
- Classroom environment
- Instruction
- Teacher responsibilities*

In selecting a topic, reflect on recent or current field experiences, personal experiences as a student, or accounts of real classroom incidents. Include some demographic data that tell a bit about the community, school, classroom, teacher, students, and curriculum. Include at least one problem for which there is no obvious answer. Use fictitious names of persons and schools to maintain confidentiality.

Your case should be approximately two pages in length (typed, double-spaced) and should include three to four Questions for Reflection, and one or two Activities for Extending Thinking. Following is a form entitled "Design Your Own Case." It outlines categories for developing your case as well as for developing criteria for assessing responses to your Questions for Reflection and your Activities for Extending Thinking.

*The four categories are from Danielson, C. (1996). *Enhancing professional practice: A framework for teaching.* Alexandria, VA: Association for Supervision and Curriculum Development.

Design Your Own Case

Author Name(s): ______________________________

Title of Case: ____________________ **Grade Level(s):** ________

Subject Matter Area (e.g., science): ____________________

Generic Teaching Topic (e.g., planning, grading): ____________________

Contextual Information:

____

Community Factors:

____

School Factors:

____

Classroom Factors:

____

Teacher Characteristics:

____

Student Characteristics:

____

Characteristics of Curriculum:

____

Story: ______________________________

____

____

____

____

Questions for Reflection:

1. ______________________________

____

2. ______________________________

____

3. ______________________________

____

Activities for Extending Thinking:

1. ____

____

2. ____

____

Criteria for assessing responses to your Questions for Reflection:

List criteria (e.g., response is clear, consistent with research or best practice, generalized to an appropriate degree—not overgeneralized, valid—based on facts in the case, relevant to an issue in the case, other).

1. ____

____

2. ____

____

Responses to Questions for Reflection:

List what you would consider to be examples of acceptable and unacceptable responses.

	Acceptable	Unacceptable
1. a.	______________	______________
b.	______________	______________
2. a.	______________	______________
b.	______________	______________
3. a.	______________	______________
b.	______________	______________

Responses to Activities for Extending Thinking:

List examples of acceptable and unacceptable responses.

1.	______________	______________
2.	______________	______________

Readings for Extending Thinking

Carnoy, M. (1994). *Faded dreams: The politics and economics of race in America.* New York: Cambridge University Press.

Davis, P. (1995). *If you came this way: A journey through the lives of the underclass.* New York: Wiley.

Eron, L. D., Gentry, J. H., & Schlegel, P. (Eds.). (1994). *Reason to hope: A psychosocial perspective on violence and youth.* Washington, DC: American Psychological Association.

Gans, H. (1995). *The war against the poor: The underclass and antipoverty policy.* New York: Basic Books.

Hochschild, J. (1995). *Facing up to the American dream: Race, class and the soul of the nation.* Princeton, NJ: Princeton University Press.

Jencks, C., & Peterson, P. E. (Eds.). (1991). *The urban underclass.* Washington, DC: The Brookings Institute.

Kotlowitz, A. (1991). *There are no children here: The story of two boys growing up in the other America.* New York: Doubleday.

Kozol, J. (1991). *Savage inequalities: Children in America's schools.* New York: Crown.

Marable, M. (1995). *Beyond black and white: Rethinking race in American politics and society.* New York: Verso Publishers.

Oliver, M., & Shapiro, T. (1995). *Black wealth/white wealth: A new perspective on racial inequality.* New York: Routledge.

Timmer, D. A., Eitzen, D. S., & Talley, K. D. (1994). *Paths to homelessness: Extreme poverty and the urban housing crisis.* Boulder: Westview.

INTERNET SITES FOR EXTENDING THINKING

http://www.starcenter.org/documents/lowincome.htm Low income does not cause low school achievement: Creating a sense of family and respect in the school environment.

http://www.starcenter.org/priority/casestudies.htm Case studies from the national study of high-performing, high-poverty schools.

http://www.starcenter.org/documents/principal.htm Principal of national blue ribbon school says high poverty schools can excel.

http://www.teachingstrategies.com/educators/ED_news/ED_news_resilience_art.html Practicing resilience in the elementary classroom.

http://www.ed.gov/offices/OUS/PES/esed/poverty3.html Academic challenge for the children of poverty report analysis and highlights.

http://www.ed.gov/pubs/urbanhope/ Hope for urban education: A study of nine high-performing, high-poverty urban elementary schools 1999.

Part 6
Religion

Case 22

Isn't the Christmas Tree a Christian Symbol?

A classroom Christmas tree and other winter holiday symbols cause students to question the teacher's intent.

It was the first week of December. The previous day Ms. Halverson had added to her bulletin boards some holiday wishes, including "Merry Christmas," "Happy Hanukkah," and "Happy Kwanza." In addition, she had placed a two-foot-tall Christmas tree in the front corner of the room by her desk.

Several of her students had entered the room a few minutes before class was to begin. The students were of Russian, Chinese, and Egyptian heritage. They made a few comments to one another and then addressed Ms. Halverson: "Ms. Halverson, you told us to let you know if we felt that our classroom was not as inclusive as it could possibly be. Well, isn't the Christmas tree a symbol of the Christian religion?" asked Yen. "And by having a Christmas tree, aren't you emphasizing one religion over another?"

Ms. Halverson nodded as Yen spoke: "Actually, it's a pre-Christian symbol that arose in Europe. But I only meant to acknowledge it as one of the most prevalent historical and cultural symbols in the United States."

Yen responded, "So you didn't mean to promote Christianity?"

"No, not at all," replied Ms. Halverson. "I'm glad that you raised the issue. I now realize that I need to clarify for the class just what my intentions are regarding the tree. Thanks for being sensitive to those who might have other interpretations. It's exactly this kind of feedback that I need to make our class more inclusive! Perhaps you and the class can offer some other suggestions for making our room look more inclusive during the holidays." The students seemed eager to help.

Questions for Reflection

1. Should Ms. Halverson have placed a Christmas tree in her room? Why or why not?

2. How adequate was Ms. Halverson's explanation of her intent to the students? What, if anything, would make it more adequate?
3. What factors might appropriately affect a teacher's decision to display religious symbols?
4. Comment on the relationship between the teacher and Yen. What did Ms. Halverson say or do that would tend to foster a healthy relationship with him?

Activities for Extending Thinking

1. Discuss with a school administrator the policies in his/her school regarding the use or display of objects that have or could have some religious meaning. Summarize your key insights in writing.
2. List school practices with regard to religion that are allowed by law. List practices not allowed by law. Summarize your findings in writing.

Case 23

My Persuasive Essay Is "Why We Should Follow Jesus"

To foster a feeling of ownership in their persuasive essays, a teacher allows students the opportunity to choose the topic they will present to the class.

Mr. Kauls had taught middle school English for 10 years. One of his favorite units was persuasive writing. Although students were typically reluctant when it came to talking to the class, they seemed to become very motivated—even excited—to talk about something in which they truly believed. Each year in a letter to parents, Mr. Kauls made it clear that his goal was to actively involve students in the *process* of writing and speaking persuasively, not to condone the specific topic chosen. How could he? Last year students spoke on "Why Abortion Should Be Available to All," "Eliminating Affirmative Action," "Why Schools Should Put Pop Machines in Each Room," and "Evidence that the White Race Is Superior," and he certainly did not agree with the premise in all of those reports.

Of course, Mr. Kauls did his best at structuring the project for students' success. Before they presented, he modeled for the class the presentation of a piece of persuasive writing of two students from a previous year, as well as one of his own. Students could see clearly how it should be done.

In addition, Mr. Kauls collected and made written suggestions on the prewriting phase of each student's persuasive essay. After rewriting, he again collected and graded the second draft. By the time it was their turn to present orally to the class, students knew that Mr. Kauls supported their plan.

Finally, Mr. Kauls made it very clear that classmates must show the presenter the utmost respect. Consequences of showing even a hint of disrespect included detention and a phone call to their parents.

As in previous years, when Mr. Kauls first explained the assignment to the class, he had students write down the topics about which they would like to write and speak. Michael, a capable student respected by classmates for his academic and athletic abilities, as

well as for his personal qualities, listed "Why We Should Follow Jesus" as the topic of his persuasive writing and speaking project.

When it was Michael's turn to present, he began by acknowledging that he knew it was risky to write and speak about his selected topic, but that he believed it was so much more important than his alternative: "Why We Should All Visit Alaska." After introductory comments, he outlined his arguments: "First, following Jesus provides a reason for living, a purpose for life, that of caring for others. Second, following Jesus assures us of eternal life, and offers salvation. Third, following Jesus helps us cope with our daily lives. I don't know how persons handle stress without the comfort that comes through prayer." Michael continued, "Because we cannot understand all the mysteries of God, we do at times need a strong faith. Finally, Jesus is a great gift. While there have been many kings throughout history, Jesus is the only one who died for us." Michael paused for a moment, then took his seat. The class applause for his presentation was louder than it had been for the other reports.

Mr. Kauls commented that Michael's report had been well organized and clearly presented and that he had more than satisfied the criteria for a good persuasive essay.

After class Greg and Dion, two students whom Michael knew only slightly, approached Michael with smiles: "I didn't know you were a Christian. We are, too. You did a good job on your report."

"Thanks," replied Michael. "Where do you guys go to church?" They talked as they walked to their lockers. "See you tomorrow," they said as each headed off to a different classroom.

The next morning Mr. Kauls read his phone messages. One was from Mr. Warren, the father of Billy Warren, one of his students. Mr. Kauls knew that the Warrens were of the Mormon faith. The other message was from Sylvia Bernstein, mother of James. The Bernsteins were Jewish. Mr. Kauls wondered if it was a coincidence that two parents who had never contacted him before were requesting an audience the day after Michael's presentation.

After school that day Mr. Kauls' suspicions were realized. When he returned their calls, both parents questioned the propriety of allowing a student to do a persuasive essay on a religious topic. "I thought that schools were prohibited from evangelism," commented Mr. Warren.

Mr. Kauls reminded them of the letter that he had sent prior to the beginning of the new unit. His conversations with both parents seemed to quell their concerns. Yet, he could not help but wonder what else he might have done to make the persuasive essay activity more satisfactory to both students and parents.

Questions for Reflection

1. What else, if anything, would you have done to prevent or address parental concerns about evangelism in the public school classroom?
2. What limits, if any, would you have set on student choice of topic?
3. The First Amendment provides for the inclusion of certain religious references in the public schools. For example, it provides for books such as the Bible (Christianity), Tanakh (Judaism), Qur'an (Islam), or Tripitaka (Buddhism) to be used as historical or literary resources. In what other ways can religion be included in the public school classroom?
4. What practices does the Constitution prohibit with respect to religion in the public schools?
5. Identify several lesson plans in your own subject matter area that would draw on religious references.

Activities for Extending Thinking

1. Discuss the issue in this case with a practicing teacher. Elicit ideas for preventing, guiding, and responding to the series of events in the story. Inquire about similar experiences that the teacher may have had. Summarize key insights in writing.
2. Select one of the Readings for Extending Thinking at the end of this section. Outline its key claims or assertions in writing, and give a personal reaction to each.
3. Discuss with parents or teachers in your community the issue of diversity *within* a religion, (e.g., Christianity). List areas of potential conflict for students due to such diversity. Give concrete examples of problems and ways they could be addressed.

Case 24

Planning for Religious Diversity: Special Needs of Muslim Students

In light of increasing numbers of Islamic children in the nation's schools, a local teacher examines the background and special needs of her Muslim students.

Ms. Bush worked hard to be sensitive to the needs of students of diverse backgrounds. She had become aware that the fastest growing group of students in her school were of the Muslim faith. She knew that social scientists have predicted that within the next 25 years, Islam will become the second-largest religion in the United States. She also knew that over one billion people—one-fifth of the world's population—were Muslim, that about 14 percent of all immigrants entering the United States are Muslim, and that while one-third of Muslims living in the United States are African-American, several million Americans from various ethnic backgrounds have adopted the religion of Islam within the last quarter century. She was curious about the special needs and interests that the students in her classroom might have.

Ms. Bush requested and received material from her local Islamic Education Foundation Center. She read from a brochure entitled "You've Got a Muslim Child in Your Room: The Needs of Muslim Children in the Public School" (Islamic Education Foundation, 2000):

Muslim students have the following needs and requirements:

> Muslim students, from the onset of puberty, may not sit in close proximity to students of the opposite sex, and they may not interact closely with them. Thus, girls and boys should be assigned to sit near others of their own sex, and should not be assigned to group or partner activities with members of the opposite sex.

Because she was familiar with research on best teaching practice, Ms. Bush had always intentionally created heterogeneous groups with respect to gender, race, learning style, and other factors.

She wondered if her students would want to follow the guidelines stated in the brochure strictly, and if they did, how she would accommodate them.

As she read further in the brochure, she learned that Muslim students may not participate in plays, social parties, proms, dating, or other such activities that involve close interaction with the opposite sex. In addition, they may not participate in any event or activity related to Halloween, Christmas, Valentine's Day, or Easter because such events have social and religious connotations contrary to the Islamic faith. In addition, they may not pay allegiance to the flag, and they should not be asked to stand and sing the national anthem. The brochure stated also that while well-meaning educators have expressed concern for Muslim students who are "deprived" of participating in activities of their non-Muslim peers, Muslim parents love their children. Therefore, teachers should refrain from expressing well-intended but inappropriate "sympathy" or disapproval of parental requests. Ms. Bush determined that she would refer additional special-needs guidelines related to physical education and prayer in the schools to her colleagues who would be most directly affected.

Ms. Bush wondered how she should react to the information she had just read. How should the special needs of her Muslim students affect her planning for the coming fall, she mused.

Questions for Reflection

1. If you were Ms. Bush, what questions might you want to ask your students and/or their parents about the special religious needs stated in the brochure?
2. Assuming that certain parents of Muslim students are quite concerned about following the tenets/principles of their faith, and that their child is moderately concerned, how, if at all, would you accommodate the need of that student to be grouped only with persons of the same sex?
3. Would you arrange meaningful alternate activities for Muslim students who could not participate in holidays such as Christmas, Halloween, and so on? If so, what types of activities might you offer?
4. How would you respond if a Muslim parent asked that his or her child not be required to say the pledge of allegiance to the flag and/or sing the U.S. national anthem?
5. Identify other religious groups and the special needs that students of each faith might have. How might you alter your curriculum or instruction to accommodate those needs?

Activities for Extending Thinking

1. Obtain from community agencies and religious organizations information about the religious needs of students in your school. If your school does not have students from a variety of religious backgrounds, obtain information about religions with which your students will likely interact in their lives beyond P-12 schooling. In general, what types of things should students know in order to interact with others of differing religions?
2. Interview students about how schools and teachers can become more aware of special religious needs of students from diverse religious backgrounds. List practical strategies that teachers can use to accommodate students with special religious needs.
3. Interview school officials in your area about current policies and practices that relate to religious affiliation. Ask about religious issues that tend to arise more often (e.g., find out how the school or district conducts winter holiday celebrations (traditionally called "Christmas Program"). Do they read scripture, sing religious songs, display traditional and/or nontraditional scenes, etc.? Ask how the school has addressed such issues.
4. How could you integrate information about religious diversity into the discipline(s) you will teach? List specific topics that you might include in certain units you are likely to teach.

Design Your Own Case

Religion

Design a case that would help classmates explore issues related to religious diversity. The story can focus on a method or strategy related to a single subject matter area (e.g., English or social studies) or on a more generic method or strategy pertinent to a wider range of subject matter areas. Your issue might also relate to:

- Planning and preparation
- Classroom environment
- Instruction
- Teacher responsibilities*

In selecting a topic, reflect on recent or current field experiences, personal experiences as a student, or accounts of real classroom incidents. Include some demographic data that tell a bit about the community, school, classroom, teacher, students, and curriculum. Include at least one problem for which there is no obvious answer. Use fictitious names of persons and schools to maintain confidentiality. Your case should be approximately two pages in length (typed, double-spaced) and should include three to four Questions for Reflection, and one or two Activities for Extending Thinking. Following is a form entitled "Design Your Own Case." It outlines categories for developing your case as well as for developing criteria for assessing responses to your Questions for Reflection and your Activities for Extending Thinking.

*The four categories are from Danielson, C. (1996). *Enhancing professional practice: A framework for teaching.* Alexandria, VA: Association for Supervision and Curriculum Development.

Design Your Own Case

Author Name(s): ______________________________

Title of Case: ______________________ **Grade Level(s):** ________

Subject Matter Area (e.g., science): ______________________

Generic Teaching Topic (e.g., planning, grading): ______________

Contextual Information:

____

Community Factors:

____

School Factors:

____

Classroom Factors:

____

Teacher Characteristics:

____

Student Characteristics:

____

Characteristics of Curriculum:

____

Story: ______________________________________

____

____

____

____

Questions for Reflection:

1. ____

____

2. ____

____

3. ____

____

Activities for Extending Thinking:

1. ____
____
2. ____
____

Criteria for assessing responses to your Questions for Reflection:

List criteria (e.g., response is clear, consistent with research or best practice, generalized to an appropriate degree—not overgeneralized, valid—based on facts in the case, relevant to an issue in the case, other).

1. ____
____
2. ____
____

Responses to Questions for Reflection:

List what you would consider to be examples of acceptable and unacceptable responses.

	Acceptable	Unacceptable
1. a.	________________	________________
b.	________________	________________
2. a.	________________	________________
b.	________________	________________
3. a.	________________	________________
b.	________________	________________

Responses to Activities for Extending Thinking:

List examples of acceptable and unacceptable responses.

1.	________________	________________
2.	________________	________________

Readings for Extending Thinking

Al-Ani, S. H. (1995). Muslims in America and Arab Americans. In C. L. Bennett (Ed.), *Comprehensive multicultural education: Theory and practice* (3rd ed., p. 139). Boston: Allyn & Bacon.

Crim, K., Bullard, R., & Shinn, L. D. (Eds.). (1981). *The perennial dictionary of world religions.* San Francisco: HarperCollins.

Feingold, H. L. (1995). *Bearing witness: How America and its Jews responded to the Holocaust.* Syracuse, NY: Syracuse University Press.

First Amendment to the Constitution of the United States, 1791.

Haltom, B. (2000). I'll keep praying for my football team. *Tennessee Bar Journal, 36*(8), 34–35.

Holliday, L. (1995). *Children in the Holocaust and WWII: Their secret diaries.* New York: Pocket Books.

Islamic Education Foundation. (2000). *You've got a Muslim child in your room: The needs of Muslim children in the public school.* Islamic Education Foundation, 2525 East Franklin Avenue, Minneapolis, MN 55406.

Kirmani, M. H., & Laster, B. P. (1999). Responding to religious diversity in classrooms. *Educational Leadership, 56*(7), 61–63.

Lustig, A. (1995). *Children of the Holocaust.* Evanston, IL: Northwestern University Press.

Markowitz, R. J. (1993). *My daughter, the teacher: Jewish teachers in the New York City schools.* New Brunswick, NJ: Rutgers University Press.

Marks, J. (1993). *The hidden children: Secret survivors of the Holocaust.* New York: Ballantine.

Marty, W. R. (1998). Christians in the academy: Overcoming the silence. *Journal of Interdisciplinary Studies, 10*(1–2), 1–16.

Not the Last Word. (2000). *America, 183*(2), 3.

Ooka Pang, V., & Barba, R. H. (1995). The power of culture: Building culturally affirming instruction. In C. A. Grant (Ed.), *Educating for diversity: An anthology of multicultural voices* (pp. 345–356). Boston: Allyn & Bacon.

Rabinove, S. (2000). The 10 Commandments and public schools: Shall we post the penalties too? *Church & State, 53*(10), 21.

Scherer, M. M. (1998). Linking education with the spiritual. *Educational Leadership, 56*(4), 5.

Smith, J. Z., & Green, W. S. (Eds.). (1995). *The HarperCollins dictionary of religion.* San Francisco: HarperCollins.

Uphoff, J. K. (1993). Religious diversity and education. In J. A. Banks & C. A. McGee Banks (Eds.), *Multicultural education: Issues and perspectives* (2nd ed., p. 46). Boston: Allyn & Bacon.

Werner, H. (1992). *Fighting back: A memoir of Jewish resistance in WW II.* New York: Columbia University Press.

Wiesel, E. (1986). *Night* (25th anniv. ed.). New York: Bantam.

Internet Sites for Extending Thinking

http://www.nmajh.org Virtual tours of online exhibitions, comparative timeline that tracks U.S. history, U.S. Jewish history, and world Jewish history.

http://www.pbs.org/echoes Illuminates historical events, shows artifacts of digs, and provides resources for classroom discussion.

http://www.jewishholidays.org Uses Jewish holidays as a way to start to talk about Jewish history and culture.

http://www.clsnet.org Christian Legal Society Web site on religious expression in public schools.

http://www.nsba.org National School Board Web site on religious expression in schools.

http://www.academicinfo.net/religindex.html Libraries, directories, and other resources on a wide variety of religions.

http://www.academicinfo.net/Religiontolerance.html References on religious tolerance/freedom.

http://www.looksmart.com Click on "Religion & Belief," click on "Islam," click on "Education," and finally click on "Online Courses."

Part 7

Special Needs

Case 25

We Only Meant It as a Joke

Several students "play a joke" on a female classmate by telling a learning-disabled pupil that she has a crush on him.

Mr. Carr consistently demonstrated respect for all his students. All students, including special-needs students, had a chance to work in heterogeneous, cooperative groups, share leadership roles, and generally contribute equally to classroom life. Mr. Carr was careful to praise and encourage all students equally.

One of the classroom procedures posted on the front wall was "Respect others." Students understood what this meant—they had been given numerous specific examples on the first day of class.

For the first six weeks of the term, Mr. Carr's students honored the procedures listed. Then one day, several students were moved to have what they considered fun with Mia, one of their classmates. They suggested to Mike, a learning-disabled student, that Mia had expressed an interest in him and that he should call her and ask her to be his girlfriend. They intended that the "joke" would be on Mia. That evening Mike called Mia. Mia politely replied that she did not want a boyfriend.

When Mr. Carr heard what had happened, he immediately thought about how he would enforce the classroom rule that students respect others. Of course, the perpetrators would have to pay the consequences established on the first day of school. Mr. Carr believed in being consistent in maintaining standards for behavioral conduct. Now he was faced with the question of how to best make this situation a learning experience.

Questions for Reflection

1. Is it possible for a teacher to establish, ahead of time, rules and consequences for an offense such as the one in this case?
2. What consequence(s) would be appropriate for the students who created the problem for Mike and Mia?
3. What might you say to Mike that would be helpful to him? What would be some responses that you would not want to make? Write out your responses.

4. What would you say to Mia? What would be some responses you would not want to make?
5. What could Mr. Carr do to help all of his students be more respectful of those with special needs?

Activities for Extending Thinking

1. Discuss with at least one special-education teacher the types of conflicts that most often occur between students with special needs and (a) teachers and (b) regular education students. What can teachers do to prevent such problems?
2. Discuss with a special-needs student what he or she would like general education teachers to do to improve interaction between special-needs students and (a) nonspecial-needs students and (b) teachers. Summarize your findings in writing and be prepared to share in class.

Case 26

Structuring for Success in a Mainstreamed Classroom

By employing a number of special instructional strategies, a teacher tries to ensure that students with learning disabilities will succeed.

Mr. French believed that mainstreaming students with mental and physical disabilities would benefit not only those with the disability but the nondisabled as well. Over the past four years, he had given much thought to how best to arrange his instruction to ensure that both groups of students would learn. With the disabled students, for example, he regularly limited problems so that they focused their learning on a single concept, included in assignments only material that was essential to the task at hand, and collected student work as soon as it was completed so that he could give immediate feedback. In addition, he held frequent, short, one-on-one conferences in which he asked each student to restate his or her responsibilities with respect to the assignment. Finally, he had a corner of his room set aside for mainstreamed students so that they could choose to work in a quiet, uncrowded area, and they frequently took advantage of the opportunity he provided.

On the third day of school, Mr. French was planning his lesson for the next day. His goal was for students to learn a number of social skills that they could use in his class, as well as in others. He would begin with listening skills and skills for asking questions, for these were two skill groups with which learning-disabled (LD), attention deficit/hyperactive disorder (ADHD), and other disabled and nondisabled students often had trouble. He would have students work in groups of five. There were five learning-disabled students in his class this term, and he would have them form one group. Mr. French reasoned that having them work together would give each student a feeling of support, knowing that each had a learning disability and no one would make fun of them. Once the groups were formed, he would briefly define and model for them one of the four good listening skills: paraphrasing, empathizing, asking open questions, and asking clarifying questions, and then he would allow them

to practice each skill through role play. If he modeled one skill at a time, students would be able to focus on that skill and not be confused with too many new concepts at once. After the groups were finished practicing the skills, the class as a large group would discuss the effects of the role play—for example, whether it was easier or harder to use the skills than they had expected and what problems they had experienced.

Each previous year, the students had seemed to enjoy the role-play activity. Mr. French always believed that students had achieved their goals in the activity.

Questions for Reflection

1. Which of the learning activities used by Mr. French would you support as being consistent with his goal of maximizing learning for both the disabled and nondisabled students? Why? Which would you oppose? Why?
2. Was Mr. French's grouping strategy appropriate and suitable for both disabled and nondisabled students? Give evidence from research to support your answer.
3. How can teachers organize the physical space in the classroom to facilitate learning for a diverse student population? Consider factors such as arrangement of furniture, use of teaching aids (e.g., overheads, flip charts, and computer presentation programs), and student accessibility to learning resources.

Activities for Extending Thinking

1. Discuss with at least two special-education teachers pedagogical techniques appropriate for students with various types of special needs. List grouping strategies, common sources of student error, and proven subject-based pedagogy for each kind of special need. In addition to identifying patterns of learning for each group, identify individual differences within those patterns. Provide demographic data on the number of students in special education in their school, including the number of males, females, students of color, and bilingual students, as well as the number mainstreamed.
2. Using written resources or special-education teachers, identify strategies for grading special-needs students. Summarize your findings in two to three pages.
3. Identify steps that teachers and other school personnel could take to advocate for students whose parents refuse to have them tested and/or admitted into a special-needs program.

Case 27

Anthony, Please Don't Push: Designing an IEP

A special-education teacher offers help in diagnosing classroom behavior of a student with special needs and in designing an appropriate Individualized Education Program (IEP) for him and for others.

Ms. Melby was an experienced special-education teacher. She loved working with special-needs students and was an ardent advocate for them. She believed in working closely with regular-education teachers who had mainstreamed students in their classrooms.

During her third-hour preparation period, Ms. Shilala, a fourth-year teacher, entered Ms. Melby's room. "Got a minute?" she asked.

Ms. Melby replied, "Yes, of course. Come in."

Ms. Shilala proceeded. "I'd like to ask you about Anthony Martinez. I believe he is in your special-ed class, is he not?"

"Yes—he's a hard worker," replied Ms. Melby.

"He's generally cooperative and pretty thorough in his work for me, too," agreed Ms. Shilala. "But one thing I don't understand is that he has a bad habit of pushing his classmates. It doesn't matter who it is. In fact, he pushes those he considers to be his friends more than anyone else. He'll be getting along fine with them and then, all of a sudden, he pushes."

"Yes," said Ms. Melby, "I think I know why. Anthony recently has been diagnosed with a vision problem. He can't see things close to him. He pushes things away, even people, so that he can see them more clearly. I've been working with him on that. You might want to explain the situation to your students. I'd also recommend that you remind him not to push, but also to ask others to step back."

"That explains it!" sighed Ms. Shilala. "I knew he wasn't a malicious kid! Thank you." After a moment, she asked, "While I'm here, may I ask one more question?"

"Sure," said Ms. Melby with a smile.

"I'm meeting tomorrow with a team to design an Individualized Education Program for Anthony. I expect his parents, social worker,

doctor, the school nurse, and Ms. Hanson, our new special-ed teacher, to attend. What are the key issues to build into the plan from a teacher's point of view?"

"Well," said Ms. Melby, "I like to consider individual style. Is the student a visual learner and perhaps one who sees the big picture; that is, a global learner? Is he or she one who learns best from manipulating concrete objects, or are abstract ideas preferred? I also think the Howard Gardner concept of multiple intelligences is important—that is, does a given pupil seem to be more able to handle ideas analytically or logically? Is he or she pretty adept interpersonally or intrapersonally? How about kinesthetic or other abilities?"

"That's a lot to think about, especially when I have six students who need IEPs!" said Ms. Shilala in a worried tone. "I don't know if I can handle six different plans that require that much detail!"

"I'd be happy to help you," said Ms. Melby. "I know quite a bit about each of them already."

"Oh, great. I'd appreciate that," sighed Ms. Shilala.

Questions for Reflection

1. What is the "moral of the story" about Anthony? In other words, what general principle(s) should we develop to help us deal with apparent misbehavior in a classroom?
2. Does Ms. Melby's advice regarding how to handle Anthony seem appropriate? What, if anything, would you change?
3. Assess Ms. Melby's response regarding the development of IEPs. What, if anything, would you change?
4. What other issues regarding the behavior of students with special needs is a concern to you?
5. Positive relationships with colleagues can benefit students as well as teachers. How can you foster collegial relationships that would benefit students with special needs?
6. What can schools do to provide more effective programs and services for pupils with special needs?

Activities for Extending Thinking

1. Talk with a student identified as having special needs. Include students with physical and mental challenges as well as those with inherited or acquired crack cocaine addictions or AIDS. Discuss those needs being met by the school as well as those that could be better met.
2. Discuss with school officials methods of diagnosing special-needs students. Inquire about the assessment instruments used

and the persons who make the decisions about classifying students as culturally and linguistically diverse (CLD). Summarize your findings in writing. Include a comment on the degree to which the evaluators are sensitive to minority and majority students, and the degree to which the evaluators are willing to assume an advocacy role for CLD students.

3. Interview a special-education teacher about specific methods regular education teachers might use to meet the special needs of students.

Design Your Own Case

Special Needs

Design a case that would help classmates explore issues related to exceptionality in schools. The story can focus on a method or strategy related to a single subject matter area (e.g., English or social studies) or on a more generic method or strategy pertinent to a wider range of subject matter areas. Your issue might also relate to:

- Planning and preparation
- Classroom environment
- Instruction
- Teacher responsibilities*

In selecting a topic, reflect on recent or current field experiences, personal experiences as a student, or accounts of real classroom incidents. Include some demographic data that tell a bit about the community, school, classroom, teacher, students, and curriculum. Include at least one problem for which there is no obvious solution. Use fictitious names of persons and schools to maintain confidentiality. Your case should be approximately two pages in length (typed, double-spaced) and should include three to four Questions for Reflection, and one or two Activities for Extending Thinking. Following is a form entitled "Design Your Own Case." It outlines categories for developing your case, as well as for developing criteria for assessing responses to your Questions for Reflection and your Activities for Extending Thinking.

*The four categories are from Danielson, C. (1996). *Enhancing professional practice: A framework for teaching.* Alexandria, VA: Association for Supervision and Curriculum Development.

Design Your Own Case

Author Name(s): ______________________________

Title of Case: ____________________ **Grade Level(s):** ________

Subject Matter Area (e.g., science): ____________________

Generic Teaching Topic (e.g., planning, grading): ____________________

Contextual Information:

____

Community Factors:

____

School Factors:

____

Classroom Factors:

____

Teacher Characteristics:

____

Student Characteristics:

____

Characteristics of Curriculum:

____

Story: ______________________________

____

____

____

____

Questions for Reflection:

1. ______________________________

____

2. ______________________________

____

3. ______________________________

____

Activities for Extending Thinking:

1. ____

____

2. ____

____

Criteria for assessing responses to your Questions for Reflection:

List criteria (e.g., response is clear, consistent with research or best practice, generalized to an appropriate degree—not overgeneralized, valid—based on facts in the case, relevant to an issue in the case, other).

1. ____

____

2. ____

____

Responses to Questions for Reflection:

List what you would consider to be examples of acceptable and unacceptable responses.

	Acceptable	Unacceptable
1. a.	____________________	____________________
b.	____________________	____________________
2. a.	____________________	____________________
b.	____________________	____________________

Responses to Activities for Extending Thinking:

List examples of acceptable and unacceptable responses.

1.	____________________	____________________
2.	____________________	____________________

Readings for Extending Thinking

Artiles, A. J., & Tvent, S. C. (1994). Overrepresentation of minority students in special education: A continuing debate. *The Journal of Special Education, 27,* 410–437.

Carrasquillo, A. L., & Rodriguez, V. (1995). *Language minority students in the mainstream classroom.* Bristol, PA: Taylor & Francis.

Correa, V. I., & Heward, W. L. (2000). Special education in a culturally diverse society. In W. L. Heward, *Exceptional children: An introduction to special education* (6th ed., pp. 82–114). Upper Saddle River, NJ: Merrill/Prentice Hall.

Ford, D. Y. (1998). The underrepresentation of minority students in gifted education: Problems and promises in recruitment and retention. *Journal of Special Education, 32,* 4–14.

Fuchs, D., & Fuchs, L. S. (1995). Sometimes separate is better. *Educational Leadership, 52*(4), 22–25.

Giangreco, M. F., Cloniger, C. J., & Iverson, V. S. (1998). *Choosing options and accommodations for children: A guide to educational planning for students with disabilities* (2nd ed.). Baltimore: MD: Paul H. Brookes.

Gottlieb, J., & Atter, M. (1995) *Overrepresentation of children of color referred to special education.* New York: New York University Department of Teaching and Learning.

Heward, W. L. (1996). *Exceptional children: An introduction to special education* (5th ed.). Upper Saddle River, NJ: Merrill/Prentice Hall.

Hill, J. L. (1999). *Meeting the needs of students with special physical and health care needs.* Upper Saddle River, NJ: Merrill/Prentice Hall.

Individuals with Disabilities Act of 1990. (1990). P.L. No 101–476, 20 U.S.C. 1400–1485.

Janney, R. E., Snell, M. E., Beers, M. K., & Raynes, M. (1995). Integrating students with moderate and severe disabilities into general education classes. *Exceptional Children, 61*(5), 425–439.

Kauffman, J. M., & Hallahan, D. K. (1995). *The illusion of full inclusion: A comprehensive critique of a current special education bandwagon.* Austin, TX: PRO-ED.

Meyer, L. H., & Park, H. S. (1999). Contemporary most promising practices for people with disabilities. In J. S. Scotti & L. H. Meyer (Eds.), *Behavioral intervention: Principles, models, and practices* (pp. 25–45). Baltimore, MD: Paul H. Brookes Publishing.

Oswald, D. P., Coutinho, M. J., Best, A. M., & Singh, N. N. (1999). Ethnic representation in special education: The influence of school-related economic and demographic variables. *The Journal of Special Education, 32,* 194–206.

Rainforth, B., York, J., & MacDonald, C. (1992). *Collaborative teams for students with severe disabilities: Integrating therapy and educational services.* Baltimore, MD: Paul H. Brookes.

Ryba, K., Selby, L., & Nolan, P. (1995). Computers empower students with special needs. *Educational Leadership, 53*(2), 82-87.

Sapon-Shevin, M. (1999). *Because we can change the world: A practical guide to building cooperative, inclusive classroom communities.* Boston: Allyn & Bacon.

Trent, S. C., Artiles, A. J., & Englert, C. S. (1998). From deficit thinking to social constructivism: A review of theory, research, and practice in special education. In *Review of research in education, 23* (pp. 277-307). Washington, DC: American Educational Research Association.

Yell, M. L. (1995). Least restrictive environment, inclusion, and students with disabilities: A legal analysis. *Journal of Special Education, 28,* 389-404.

Internet Sites for Extending Thinking

http://ericec.org Sponsored by the Educational Resources Information Center (ERIC), this site is a clearinghouse for data on the disabilities and gifted education. The site features links to webpages containing fact sheets, digests, laws, research, and other subjects, as well as to online discussions groups, an FAQ, and databases relevant to the subject.

http://www.ldonline.org/ This site, run by the Learning Project at WETA, offers a wealth of information, via internal links to numerous data pages, on various LDs themselves, the issues surrounding LD in education, and other information. In addition, you can take part in online discussion, sign up for a free online newsletter, or submit questions about LDs.

http://seriweb.com Billed as "Special Education Resources on the Internet," SERI is basically an extensive page of links to more links, covering almost every aspect of special education. From legal issues to definitions of various disabilities, discussion groups, organization listings - if there's a Web site covering some aspect of special education, you will doubtless find it here on one of the many secondary pages.

http://www.educationworld.com/special_ed/ Education World brings you this megasite which contains a vast assortment of special education information that is both wide and deep: Articles (including an archive), reviews, resource listings, databases, reference centers, and more. The site is a breeze to navigate and easy to read.

http://www.cec.sped.org/index.html Council for Exceptional Children site includes publications and products, professional standards, discussion forums, a link to ERIC Clearinghouse on disabilities and gifted education, career connections, and professional development training events, all on topics relating to exceptionality.

http://hoagiesgifted.org Click on "educators" for information on books, programs, curriculum, and theories on gifted education.

Part 8

Affectional Orientation

Case 28

Not in My Group—He's Gay!

A student publicly objects to the inclusion of a classmate in his small group because, he claims, the classmate is "gay."

Ms. Collins was a firm believer in education that is multicultural and has the potential to lead to social reform. She organized her curriculum around issues of race, gender, class, disability, language, and affectional orientation. She used the lives of students in her classes as the starting point for addressing such issues.

On this day Ms. Collins' students were busily engaged in small group discussions about their family heritage projects. She had asked students to share the information about their ethnic heritage that they had obtained from their parents or guardians the night before. Ms. Collins hoped that not only would the small group discussions give her pupils opportunities to express themselves, but they might also help identify differences and similarities among classmates. Further, she thought the discussions would help them be more thoughtful about what else they would need to find out to make their projects more complete.

As she moved to the small group of students in the rear of the room, Xeng, a Hmong student new to the class, said to her as he pointed to a classmate named Kim, "I don't want him in my group. He's gay!" The other group members covered their mouths and laughed.

Ms. Collins was caught by surprise. Consistent enforcement of class rules established at the beginning of the school year had prevented the use of such labels in her class until today. She noticed that Kim appeared embarrassed by Xeng's accusation.

"Do you know what 'gay' means?" she asked, in an effort to determine if Xeng was just repeating something he had heard someone else say, without knowing what it meant.

"Yes," replied Xeng. "It's when one man has sex with another man."

Ms. Collins was baffled. She thought to herself, "Should I ask if Xeng is sure, or how he knows that Kim is gay? Should I ask Xeng if he is angry with Kim, and, if so, why? Should I reprimand Xeng for making his judgment public? How should I respond to Kim?"

Ms. Collins was aware of the tremendous controversy over the inclusion in many schools across the country of GLBT (Gay, Lesbian, Bisexual, Transgendered) issues in the classroom. She would review the school policy and would discuss the matter with the principal.

Questions for Reflection

1. List possible factors that may have motivated Xeng to say what he said about Kim. What personal needs might Xeng have been trying to satisfy?
2. Write several sentences illustrating how you would handle the situation. Would you respond differently (a) if Xeng were not a new student, (b) if Xeng were not Hmong, or (c) if Xeng had personal problems at home?
3. Knowing that the word "gay" is often used as a derogatory term, under what conditions, if any, would you involve the class in a discussion of this issue? Write down the actual opening statements/questions you would use to introduce such a discussion.
4. What other incidents regarding affectional preference have you observed in schools? How were they addressed? How should they have been addressed?

Activities for Extending Thinking

1. Discuss with an experienced practicing teacher the strategies he or she uses to create and maintain a safe classroom environment for all students. List those strategies in writing and be prepared to share in class.
2. Interview an advocate for gay, lesbian, bisexual, and transgendered students to identify key issues and specific strategies that classroom teachers can use to create a safe, inclusive environment.
3. Talk with a gay, lesbian, bisexual, or transgendered student regarding classroom incidents experienced by him or her, or by friends who are GLBT. Elicit recommendations for preventing negative experiences and encouraging positive ones.
4. Discuss with a principal or superintendent the school and district policies regarding the inclusion of GLBT issues in their schools.

Case 29

In Islam, Homosexuality Is a Sin and a Crime

A student confides in her class that she is lesbian, and a Muslim student states that homosexuality is a sin and a crime in Islam.

Ms. Elness worked hard to develop an inclusive classroom. She believed in honoring cultural diversity, in designing multicultural curricula, and, in general, running a student-centered classroom. Because they knew she cared about all students, her pupils trusted her.

As part of her service to the school, Ms. Elness served as faculty sponsor of the Gay, Lesbian, Bisexual, Transgendered (GLBT) support group that met bimonthly after school. She recalled that three years ago when she volunteered to sponsor the group, she had been nervous. Each year, however, her work as an advocate for students in the GLBT group had become more and more gratifying.

In addition to providing a forum for GLBT students to socialize and to discuss important issues, Ms. Elness would meet with other faculty to help them understand the general and specific needs of students in the group. Each year, on the first day of class, in her own classes she would discuss her work with the group so that students would know of her belief in the importance of creating a safe environment for all.

It was the sixth week of the school year. Ms. Elness had distributed newspapers and asked students to read and summarize for the class a news report of a current event. Tyrone reported an incident on a local university campus in which a number of students had harassed and physically beaten a student because he was gay.

Robert responded to the report, "I don't think that happens that much anymore. Most people are more accepting of people who are different."

Margie raised her hand. "I disagree," she said. "I'm a lesbian, and when people find out, they often look at me funny or avoid me entirely."

Ms. Elness was somewhat surprised. Margie had not confided in her, or as far as she knew in anyone else in the school, about her affectional orientation.

Before Ms. Elness could respond, Fahid, a Muslim student, said in a calm, informing tone of voice, "In Islam, it is a sin and crime to practice homosexuality. Those who believe in Islam know they will be punished if they are found to be homosexual."

Ms. Elness sensed that Fahid was intending merely to describe a belief system held by Muslim people, not to demean Margie. At the same time, his comments seemed ill timed, for Margie had taken a risk to share her secret with the class, only to be informed that her disposition was considered a sin and a crime by a formidable group of people. Several students rolled their eyes, as if to suggest that Fahid was expressing a narrow point of view, was being intolerant, or at least was out of line. Mark verbalized their dissatisfaction in a disgusted tone of voice: "That's only the opinion of one religion—it doesn't mean it actually is a sin or a crime—only that one religion thinks it is."

Jennifer cautioned Mark and the others who had rolled their eyes, "Let's remember now that Fahid is describing for us another cultural perspective. We ought not judge him for helping us to understand another point of view."

Noting that there was only a minute left in the period, Ms. Elness interrupted, "Yes, I appreciate the comments of both Margie and Fahid. And Jennifer is right—we must acknowledge the right of both Margie and Fahid to hold the beliefs that they hold." She had barely finished when the bell rang.

As the students filed out, she wondered, "How should I follow-up with Fahid, Margie, Mark, and Jennifer? Should we follow-up in class tomorrow, or go on with the next lesson in the unit plan?"

Questions for Reflection

1. In your opinion, how should Ms. Elness follow-up with
   a. Margie
   b. Fahid
   c. Mark
   d. Jennifer
   e. the class
   f. others (identify)
2. What, if any, are the positive aspects of this case?
3. If you were the teacher, what might you have done differently to prevent, guide, or correct inappropriate student behaviors?
4. What assumptions had Mark made about Fahid's comments? Do they seem warranted?

Activities for Extending Thinking

1. Discuss with a gay, lesbian, bisexual, or transgendered student his or her school experience. Inquire about what the school is currently doing and what else, if anything, it could do to provide a safe, inclusive environment for GLBT students.
2. List specific steps you can take to better advocate for a safe environment for all students, particularly those who are GLBT.
3. Develop a list of curriculum resources that include gay, lesbian, bisexual, or transgendered persons and issues that could be used at the grade level at which you teach. Include several nonfiction and fiction resources.
4. Discuss with a school administrator, a principal, or superintendent their school and district policies on the inclusion of GLBT issues.

 DESIGN YOUR OWN CASE 

Affectional Orientation

Design a case that explores an issue of affectional orientation in the classroom. The story can focus on a method or strategy related to a single subject matter area (e.g., English or social studies) or on a more generic method or strategy pertinent to a wider range of subject matter areas. Your issue might also relate to:

- Planning and preparation
- Classroom environment
- Instruction
- Teacher responsibilities*

In selecting a topic, reflect on recent or current field experiences, personal experiences as a student, or accounts of real classroom incidents. Include some demographic data that tell a bit about the community, school, classroom, teacher, students, and curriculum. Include at least one problem for which there is no obvious solution. Use fictitious names of persons and schools to maintain confidentiality. Your case should be approximately two pages in length (typed, double-spaced) and should include three to four Questions for Reflection, and one or two Activities for Extending Thinking. Following is a form entitled "Design Your Own Case." It outlines categories for developing your case, as well as for developing criteria for assessing responses to your Questions for Reflection and your Activities for Extending Thinking.

*The four categories are from Danielson, C. (1996). *Enhancing professional practice: A framework for teaching.* Alexandria, VA: Association for Supervision and Curriculum Development.

Design Your Own Case

Author Name(s): ______________________________

Title of Case: ____________________ **Grade Level(s):** ________

Subject Matter Area (e.g., science): ____________________

Generic Teaching Topic (e.g., planning, grading): ______________

Contextual Information:

____

Community Factors:

____

School Factors:

____

Classroom Factors:

____

Teacher Characteristics:

____

Student Characteristics:

____

Characteristics of Curriculum:

____

Story: ______________________________

____

____

____

____

Questions for Reflection:

1. ______________________________

____

2. ______________________________

____

3. ______________________________

____

Activities for Extending Thinking:

1. ____

____

2. ____

____

Criteria for assessing responses to your Questions for Reflection:

List criteria (e.g., response is clear, consistent with research or best practice, generalized to an appropriate degree—not overgeneralized, valid—based on facts in the case, relevant to an issue in the case, other).

1. ____

____

2. ____

____

Responses to Questions for Reflection:

List what you would consider to be examples of acceptable and unacceptable responses.

	Acceptable	Unacceptable
1. a.	____________	____________
b.	____________	____________
2. a.	____________	____________
b.	____________	____________

Responses to Activities for Extending Thinking:

List examples of acceptable and unacceptable responses.

1.	____________	____________
2.	____________	____________

Readings for Extending Thinking

Bass, E., & Kaufman, K. (1996). *Free your mind: The book for gay, lesbian and bisexual youth—and their allies.* New York: HarperPerennial.

Butler, K. L., & Byrne, T. J. (1992). Homophobia among preservice elementary teachers. *Journal of Health Education, 23*(6), 357–358.

Cowan, T. (1992). *Gay men and women who enriched the world.* Boston: Alyson.

Harbeck, K. M. (Ed.). (1992). *Coming out of the classroom closet: Gay and lesbian students, teachers, and curricula.* Binghamton, NY: Haworth.

Herdt, G., & Boxer, A. (1993). *Children of horizons: How gay and lesbian teens are leading a new way out of the closet.* Boston: Beacon Press.

Hutchins, L., & Kaahumanu, L. (Eds.). (1991). *Bi any other name: Bisexual people speak out.* Boston: Alyson.

Jennings, K. (1994). *Becoming visible: A reader of gay and lesbian history for high school and college students.* Boston: Alyson.

Remafedi, G. (Ed.). (1994). *Death by denial: Studies of suicide in gay and lesbian teenagers.* Boston: Alyson.

Williams, K., Doyle, M., Taylor, B., & Ferguson, G. (1992). Addressing sexual orientation in a public high school. *Journal of School Health, 62*(4), 154–156.

INTERNET SITES FOR EXTENDING THINKING

http://www.glsen.org Site of national organization fighting to end anti-gay bias in K-12 schools.

http://www.pflag.org Links to resources on relationships, anti-gay hate crimes; bibliography—by Parents, Families, and Friends of Lesbians and Gays.

PART 9

LANGUAGE

Case 30

You'll Need Both Black Vernacular and Standard English

A teacher considers varying opinions from colleagues regarding the acceptance of student use of Black English Vernacular.

Mr. Drake had corrected the creative writing homework assignment from the previous day. He had wrestled with one particular paper written by Matt Williams, an African-American student who was new to the school. Mr. Drake was unsure how to handle Matt's use of Black English Vernacular (BEV). Throughout the paper were statements in which "be" was used as a finite verb, statements such as "He be happy and nice," and "When they both be home, they usually be working around the house." And there were other differences in the use of grammar, differences such as using "done" to note that an action had been completed, as in "She done finished it"; the use of double or triple negatives, as in "They ain't got no car"; and the use of "f" for "th" as in "wif" for with.

At lunch Mr. Drake approached Ms. Grover, a trusted colleague in the classroom next to him. He showed her Matt's paper. Ms. Grover read several paragraphs and said, "If I were you, I'd tell him that if I accepted this form of language, he would never learn to operate in society—that he would be at a disadvantage when applying for jobs. Moreover, I'd tell him that Black English Vernacular is a deviation from correct, standard English." Mr. Drake thanked her for her advice.

Mr. Drake also shared his problem with Ms. Manning. He knew she was taking a continuing education course on sociolinguistics at a nearby college. She was interested in his dilemma.

"Would you like to hear a few lines about dialects from our course text?" she asked. Mr. Drake nodded affirmatively. Ms. Manning read from her textbook:

> The fact is, however, that standard English is only one variety among many, although a peculiarly important one. Linguistically speaking, it cannot even legitimately be considered better than other varieties. The scientific study of all language has convinced scholars that all languages, and correspondingly all dialects, are equally "good" as linguistic systems. All varieties of a language are

> structured, complex, rule-governed systems that are wholly adequate for their speakers.... There is nothing at all inherent in nonstandard varieties that makes them inferior. Any apparent inferiority is due only to their association with speakers from underprivileged, low-status groups.*

When she had finished reading, she told Mr. Drake of three students in her classes, each of whom used a different form of BEV. She explained to him that Amy, from New York, might say, for example, "Let's get ready to roll to the store," while Darnelle, a white student from Georgia, might say, "Let's be fiddin [fixing] to go to tha sto," and Dion, from Louisiana, would likely say, "We goin to make groceries." It was clear to Mr. Drake that black English varied by region, depending on the cultural context in which it was learned and used.

Mr. Drake thanked Ms. Manning for her comments. On his way home from school, Mr. Drake wondered how he should respond to Matt's use of black English in his paper.

Questions for Reflection

1. What other information, if any, would you need in order to decide how you would respond to Matt?
2. Write verbatim how you would begin a conversation with Matt about his use of BEV. Include specific comments about how his use of BEV will affect his grade on this assignment and on other work in your class in the future. Include elements of good feedback (i.e., it is specific, constructive, substantive, and accurate).
3. How might your response affect Matt's learning, his sense of self-worth, and the socioemotional climate of your classroom?
4. What limits, if any, would you establish regarding the use of nonstandard English in your classroom?
5. How does the cultural context of the class, school, and community affect how you would respond to Matt?
6. What principles for evaluation of language use should a teacher use?

Activity for Extending Thinking

1. Discuss with parents and teachers, including parents and teachers of color, the issue of allowing or encouraging the use of dialects in the classroom. Elicit their opinions regarding how flexible and responsive a teacher should be in accepting the use of dialects. Summarize your discussions in writing.

*Trudgill, P. (1984). *Socio-linguistics: An introduction to language and society.* New York: Penguin Books, p. 20.

Case 31

They Speak English and Spanish Well, but a Learning Disability Creates Problems in Reading and Writing

A teacher and principal discuss programs and resources for two Hispanic students, each of whom has a learning disability and limited language proficiency.

Ms. Perez was regarded by students and colleagues as a hardworking and well-respected first-year teacher at Central. She loved kids and wanted them to enjoy learning. She was warm and compassionate, had a good sense of humor, and, at the same time, was clearly in charge of her classroom. She acted quickly and fairly when her young students needed guidance or correction. She spoke both English and Spanish fluently.

Ms. Perez was committed to designing lessons that were developmentally appropriate and that reflected the culturally diverse society in which her students were likely to live. She learned quickly about the characteristics, needs, interests, and abilities of her students, and although she admitted to not having great knowledge about the many ethnicities, special abilities, and language acquisition needs of children, she worked hard at identifying resources that might supplement her knowledge.

Two of Ms. Perez's Hispanic students, Rita and Ramona, in their third year in an English-speaking school, possessed highly developed oral language skills in both English and Spanish, and a learning disability (LD) resulting in limited reading and writing abilities. Ms. Perez had made certain that the learning disability had been properly diagnosed, for she knew that academic English takes much longer than oral English to develop and that sometimes educators *assume* that any reading and writing problems are LD problems. Both of the girls had been similarly diagnosed in the Spanish-speaking school they had attended before coming to Central.

Ms. Perez aggressively supported a more holistic, student-centered collaborative approach in which the girls would be placed in a general education setting, experience an oral-based bilingual curriculum, and work on developing reading and writing in the content areas. Ms. Perez contacted special-service program personnel in bilingual and English as a Second Language (ESL) programs, special education, and counseling and worked with friends and colleagues to identify bilingual community members who could tutor the girls after school. She was indeed an advocate for culturally and linguistically diverse (CLD) students in her room.

It was in the fourth month of school when Ms. Perez had an idea that she felt needed to be discussed with the principal. One day during lunch break, she encountered Ms. Williams, the principal, in the cafeteria.

"Ms. Williams, I was wondering if it would benefit our staff and students if we were to offer some parent training programs that would improve parents' ability to help their children in reading, writing, and speaking," began Ms. Perez. "We could focus on practical interaction skills for building self-esteem and on positive approaches to learning to read and write. What do you think?"

"Sounds like a great idea!" replied Ms. Williams. "Mr. Lopez would have a lot to offer in the area of self-esteem and we could identify other Latino role models as speakers. We could also see if those who come to the first session or two would want to establish support groups—perhaps neighborhood based—to conduct ongoing discussions of our sessions and of personally relevant problems. I think it could work!"

"I think so, too," said Ms. Perez. "And perhaps later on there will be opportunities to encourage parent input on making curriculum more culturally relevant. It might be one good way of empowering parents."

"Let's bring it up at the next faculty meeting and see what we can do to move ahead. I'm all for it!" said Ms. Williams. She continued, "On a related topic, I've been wondering if Rita and Ramona should be moved to a self-contained classroom for learning-disabled students. They would be with students with similar needs and the instruction would be in English, the language in which they need the most work. What do you think?"

Ms. Perez had always thought that the current general education arrangement was the best for the two girls. At the same time, on other issues, she had usually agreed with Ms. Williams, whom she considered to be a wise administrator. Perhaps moving the girls from their current general education program into the special education class could have significant benefits for them.

Questions for Reflection

1. What thoughts and feelings do you have in response to Ms. Perez's dilemma about a general versus special-education placement for Rita and Ramona?
2. How would you respond to the principal's proposal to move the girls to a self-contained special-education classroom? Provide a rationale for your response.
3. What other school and community resources *for teachers* would be helpful in dealing with CLD students?
4. What other school and community resources for *CLD students* would be helpful?
5. What suggestions would you have for modifying or expanding Ms. Perez's plan for a parent-education program?

Activities for Extending Thinking

1. Identify specific school and community resources available in a school in your area (perhaps a school in which you are currently involved in a field experience, or in which you are teaching) for CLD students and for students of other traditionally underrepresented groups.
2. Identify parent-education programs in a local school (perhaps a school in which you are in a field experience or in which you are teaching). Briefly describe their goals, methods, and evidence of progress toward their goals.
3. Identify and interpret legal aspects of bilingual and special education, including major civil rights legislation, the Bilingual Education Act (also known as Title VII), the Individuals with Disabilities Education Act of 1990, and related case law.
4. On the Internet, explore state resources (e.g., state departments of education) and national resources for teachers and for students (e.g., U.S. Department of Education: www.ed.gov/index.html) that would serve you in curriculum planning in the future. Develop a list of other Web sites, such as Administration for Children and Families: www.acf.dhhs.gov and Children Now www.dnai.com/~children. Identify and explore other such general sites as well as those more specific to the instruction of CLD students. (Because URLs are subject to change, be prepared to search for the organizations themselves.)
5. Participate in an education listserv and/or newsgroup such as edweb.cnidr.org:90/usenets.html. Keep a journal of your participation.

6. Interview a parent of a CLD student to ascertain his or her views on how the school can provide better services for the child.
7. Contact a community agency that works with CLD, ESL, or bilingual students to learn what programs are available for children and parents.

Case 32

A Bilingual Teacher's Aide Assesses His New School

A bilingual teacher's aide ponders specific strategies for helping teachers better understand their ESL and bilingual students' abilities, interests, prior knowledge, and individual needs.

It was the first day of school and Andy Seng, a bilingual teacher's aide with 10 years of experience, entered his new school building. He was excited to meet the staff and students.

He had been pleased when he attended the workshop week prior to the first week of actual classes. He had seen "Welcome" signs in several different languages posted above the doors. He had been greeted by bilingual volunteers, some of whom were students and some of whom were community members. He had noticed universal symbols and photos over important places, such as the bathrooms, cafeteria, library, and school office. He had also seen that many of the classrooms contained resource books in a number of different languages, and he had talked to teachers who said that they encouraged journal writing in the student's first language. All of these factors, he thought, would help to develop a positive atmosphere for English as a Second Language (ESL) and bilingual students.

He and the principal had decided during workshop week that it might be useful for him to shadow one or two ESL students during the first day to get an idea of school and classroom policies and practices relative to ESL and bilingual pupils. On his first day, he followed two Vietnamese students, one throughout the morning, the other during the afternoon. Both had been placed in mainstreamed classrooms taught only in English.

At the end of each half day, he spoke with each student. "How did you like your morning?" he asked the first student, whose name was Hung. "It was confusing," Hung replied. "My teacher had the class work in small groups. Since I didn't know what to do, I just watched the other students. And later on the playground, the teacher had us play softball. She thought we'd all know how, but I had never heard of softball before. I was embarrassed."

When Andy asked Chau, the student he followed during the afternoon, Chau responded, "I think my teacher thinks I'm not as smart as the others. He gave me problems that were much more simple than those he gave to the other students." Chau paused. "After class some of the kids made fun of the lunch I brought from home—that made me feel bad." Andy had worked as a teacher's aide for five years in each of two other schools. He knew that most teachers accepted, appreciated, and supported ESL and bilingual students. However, he had also seen a few teachers who had expectations that were either much too low or much too high for such students. Most cases of too-high expectations involved students of Asian heritage; cases of too-low expectations usually involved Latino or African-American students. Based on his past experience, then, Chau's situation was an exception to the rule. Andy thanked both Hung and Chau for their responses and promised both of them that he would support them and other ESL and bilingual students throughout the term.

After school that day, Andy pondered ways that he might help teachers know more about the abilities, interests, and needs of each of their ESL and bilingual students. He knew that just telling teachers in a memo or even personally would not necessarily result in their knowing students better. He knew his goal was to be an advocate for students; now he just had to identify the strategies.

Questions for Reflection

1. Andy noted some positive steps the school and some individual teachers had taken to make students of other cultures feel more at home. What were they? What else could the school have done to this end?
2. The students also mentioned some teacher behaviors that had a detrimental effect on student morale. What behaviors did they note? What would you have done differently in each case?

Teacher behaviors with detrimental effects	What I would have done
a.	a.
b.	b.
c.	c.

3. What kinds of information should teachers have about students in their classes? From what sources could they obtain each type of information?

4. Consider a similar episode involving two students of another culture or of two different cultures—for example, two Russian students, or a Muslim and an Arab student, or a Native American and a Hispanic student. What cultural issues would likely be raised?
5. What actions would you recommend that Andy take to address the problems he has encountered with Hung's and Chau's teachers? What cultural attributes must be taken into account when making these recommendations?

Activities for Extending Thinking

1. Discuss with officials of a local school the language diversity within that school. List the different languages spoken and the services for students who speak them. Include bilingual, ESL, and limited English-proficiency (LEP) services and programs.
2. Talk with a bilingual and an ESL teacher to identify methods they use to promote academic learning and language development in their classrooms. Discuss what regular-education teachers can do to help ESL, bilingual, and LEP students achieve their course goals.
3. Talk with an ESL/ELL (English Language Learners) teacher about how to address issues of working in groups, accessing prior knowledge, learning styles, and assessment as they pertain to LEP students. Summarize your key insights in writing (one to two pages).

 Design Your Own Case 

Language Diversity

Design a case that explores an issue of language diversity in the classroom. The story can focus on a method or strategy related to a single subject matter area (e.g., English or social studies) or on a more generic method or strategy pertinent to a wider range of subject matter areas. Your issue might also relate to:

- Planning and preparation
- Classroom environment
- Instruction
- Teacher responsibilities*

In selecting a topic, reflect on recent or current field experiences, personal experiences as a student, or accounts of real classroom incidents. Include some demographic data that tell a bit about the community, school, classroom, teacher, students, and curriculum. Include at least one problem for which there is no obvious solution. Use fictitious names of persons and schools to maintain confidentiality. Your case should be approximately two pages in length (typed, double-spaced) and should include three to four Questions for Reflection, and one or two Activities for Extending Thinking. Following is a form entitled "Design Your Own Case." It outlines categories for developing your case, as well as for developing criteria for assessing responses to your Questions for Reflection and your Activities for Extending Thinking.

*The four categories are from Danielson, C. (1996). *Enhancing professional practice: A framework for teaching.* Alexandria, VA: Association for Supervision and Curriculum Development.

DESIGN YOUR OWN CASE

Author Name(s): ______________________________

Title of Case: ______________________ **Grade Level(s):** ________

Subject Matter Area (e.g., science): ______________________

Generic Teaching Topic (e.g., planning, grading): ______________

Contextual Information:

____

Community Factors:

____

School Factors:

____

Classroom Factors:

____

Teacher Characteristics:

____

Student Characteristics:

____

Characteristics of Curriculum:

____

Story: ______________________________

____

____

____

____

Questions for Reflection:

1. ______________________________

____

2. ______________________________

____

3. ______________________________

____

Activities for Extending Thinking:

1. ____

____

2. ____

____

Criteria for assessing responses to your Questions for Reflection:

List criteria (e.g., response is clear, consistent with research or best practice, generalized to an appropriate degree—not overgeneralized, valid—based on facts in the case, relevant to an issue in the case, other).

1. ____

____

2. ____

____

Responses to Questions for Reflection:

List what you would consider to be examples of acceptable and unacceptable responses.

	Acceptable	Unacceptable
1. a.	____________	____________
b.	____________	____________
2. a.	____________	____________
b.	____________	____________

Responses to Activities for Extending Thinking:

List examples of acceptable and unacceptable responses.

1.	____________	____________
2.	____________	____________

 Readings for Extending Thinking 

Artiles, A. J., & Trent, S. C. (1994). Overrepresentation of minority students in special education: A continuing debate. *The Journal of Special Education, 27,* 410–437.

Baca, L. M., & Cervantes, H. T. (1989). *The bilingual special education interface* (2nd ed.). Upper Saddle River, NJ: Merrill/Prentice Hall.

Brinton, D., Goodwin, J., & Ranks, L. (1994). Helping language minority students read and write analytically: The journey into, through, and beyond. In F. Peitzman & G. Gadda (Eds.), *With different eyes* (pp. 57–88). Reading, MA: Addison Wesley Longman.

California Department of Education. (1990). *Bilingual education handbook: Designing instruction for LEP students.* Sacramento: Author.

Chan, J., & Chips, B. (1989). Helping LEP students survive in the content-area classroom. *Thrust, 18*(6), 49–51.

Clark, K. (1999). *From primary language instruction to English immersion: How five California districts made the switch.* Washington, DC: READ (Institute for Research in English Acquisition and Development).

Cummins, J. (1994). From coercive to collaborative relations of power in the teaching of literacy. In R. M. Ferdman, R. M. Weber, & A. G. Ramírez (Eds.), *Literacy across languages and cultures* (pp. 3–29). Albany: State University of New York Press.

Cummins, J. (1996). Primary language instruction and the education of language minority students. In *Schooling and language minority students: A theoretical framework* (2nd ed., pp. 3–46). Los Angeles: Evaluation, Dissemination and Assessment Center, School of Education, California State University, Los Angeles.

Cummins, J. (1999). Alternative paradigms in bilingual education research: Does theory have a place? *Educational Researcher, 28*(7), 26–34.

Cummins, J. (2000). Beyond adversarial discourse: Searching for common ground in the education of bilingual students. In C. J. Ovando & P. McLaren (Eds.), *The politics of multiculturalism and bilingual education: Students and teachers caught in the cross fire* (pp. 126–147). Boston: McGraw-Hill.

Delgado-Gaitan, C., & Trueba, H. (1991). *Crossing cultural borders.* New York: Falmer Press.

Díaz-Soto, L. (1991). Understanding bilingual/bicultural young children. *Young Children, 46*(2), 30–36.

Díaz, S., Moll, L. C., & Mehan, H. (1996). Sociocultural resources in instruction: A context-specific approach. In *Beyond language: Social and cultural factors in schooling language minority students* (pp. 187–230). Los Angeles: Evaluation, Dissemination and Assessment Center, School of Education, California State University, Los Angeles.

Ferdman, B. M., & Weber, R. M. (1994). Literacy across languages and cultures. In B. M. Ferdman, R. M. Weber, & A. G. Ramírez (Eds.), *Literacy across languages and cultures* (pp. 3–29). Albany: State University of New York Press.

Gándara, P., Maxwell-Jolly, J., García, E., Asato, J., Gutiérrez, K., Stritkus, T., & Curry, J. (2000). *The initial impact of Proposition 227 on the instruction of English learners.* Davis: University of California Linguistic Minority Research Institute.

Gersten, R. (1999). The changing face of bilingual education. *Educational Leadership, 56*(7), 41–45.

Gonzales, V., Brusca-Vega, R., & Yaukey, T. (1997). *Assessment and instruction of culturally and linguistically diverse students.* Boston: Allyn & Bacon.

Gottlieb, J., & Alter, M. (1995). *Overrepresentation of children of color referred to special education.* New York: New York University Department of Teaching Learning.

Griego-Jones, T. (1991). Rethinking programs for language minority students. *The Journal of Educational Issues of Language Minority Students, 9,* 61–74.

Gunderson, L. (1991). *ESL literacy instruction: A guidebook to theory and practice.* Englewood Cliffs, NJ: Regents/Prentice Hall.

Joyce, B. (Ed.). (1990). *Changing school culture through staff development.* Alexandria, VA: Association for Supervision and Curriculum Development.

Kuhlman, N., & Murray, D. E. (2000). Changing populations, changing needs in teacher preparation. In M.A. Snow (Ed.), *Implementing the ESL standards for pre-K-12 students through teacher education* (pp. 33–48). Alexandria, VA: Teachers of Speakers of Other Languages.

Moegher, M. E. (1995, October). Learning English on the Internet. *Educational Leadership, 53*(2), 88–90.

National Forum on Personnel Needs for Districts with Changing Demographics. (1990, May). *Staffing the multilingually impacted schools of the 1990s.* Washington, DC: U.S. Department of Education.

Nieto, S. (1992). *Affirming diversity: The sociopolitical context of multicultural education.* New York: Longman.

Ogbu, J. U. (1999). Beyond language: Ebonics, proper English, and identity in a Black-American speech community. *American Educational Research Journal, 36*(2), 147–184.

Ovando, C. J., & McLaren, P. (2000). *The politics of multiculturalism and bilingual education: Students and teachers caught in the cross fire.* Boston: McGraw-Hill.

Peregoy, S. F., & Boyle, O. F. (1993). *Reading, writing, and learning in ESL.* Reading, MA: Addison Wesley Longman.

Porter, R. P. (1999–2000). The benefits of English immersion. *Educational Leadership, 57*(4), 52–56.

Smitherman, G. (1999). *Talkin that talk: Language, culture, and education in Africa America.* New York: Routledge.

Snow, M.A. (Ed.). (2000). *Implementing the ESL standards for pre-K-12 students through teacher education.* Alexandria, VA: Teachers of Speakers of Other Languages.

Todd, L. (1997). Ebonics: An evaluation. *English Today, (13),* pp. 13–17.

INTERNET SITES FOR EXTENDING THINKING

http://members.aol.com/jakajk/ESLLessons.html Classroom resources and materials.

http:www.ncbe.gwu.edu Resources about effective education practices for culturally and linguistically diverse learners.

http://www.eslpartyland.com Lesson plans, quizzes, discussion forums, and other engaging resources.

http://www.ncbe.gwu.edu/about.htm Manuals, articles, conference announcements, bibliographies on urban education.

Part 10

Parent and Community Involvement

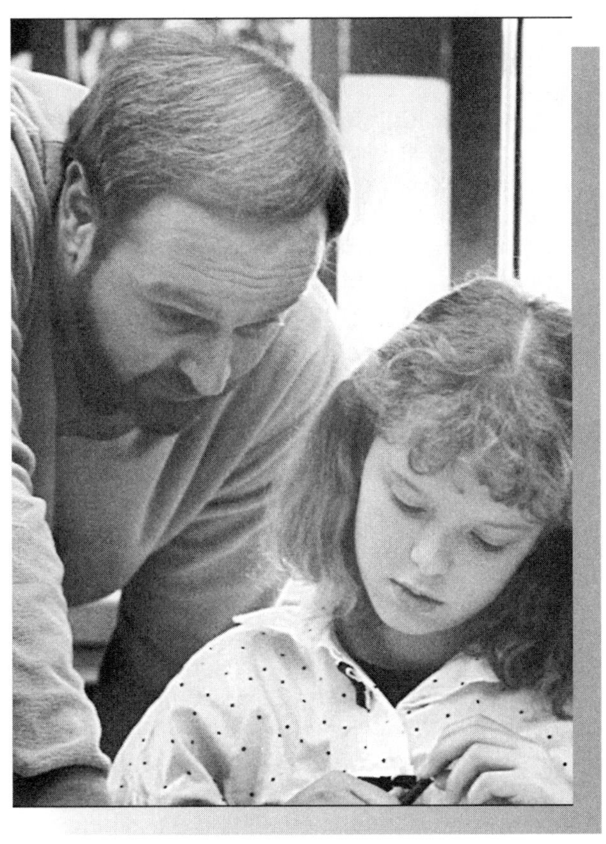

Case 33

It Takes a Village

Several teachers discuss the difficulty of getting parents involved in school. One suggests an approach that worked for him.

It was lunch hour in the faculty lounge. Mr. Jordan said to the other five teachers at his table, "I was disappointed with the turnout last night at my parent conferences. The parents of only two students attended. How many came to your conferences?"

The other teachers reported low numbers also. "The kids deserve more," one of them commented.

"I've tried everything to get parents to become more involved in the education of their children, but I've had little success," said Mr. Jordan. "Have any of you found ways to reach parents?"

Several of the teachers described the ways in which they had tried, with minimal success, to get parents to volunteer to assist with classes, assist their own children with homework, attend school events, or come to parent conferences. One teacher even held parent conferences in conference rooms and lobbies of apartment buildings in which parents lived. Still, few came. Another told of how he invited parents of other cultural backgrounds to act as translators for limited English-proficiency (LEP) students and parents, and to serve on an educational advisory committee, again with little success. Finally, Mr. Randall, the English teacher, spoke up: "For the first year ever, I have more parent volunteers to speak to my class, tutor, and act as teacher's aides than I'll ever be able to use. It's really amazing!"

"Well," asked the others, "how did you do it?"

Mr. Randall responded, "This year, for the first time, I made certain that the first communication that each parent received from me was about some talent, gift, ability, or contribution that his or her child had made to class. I assumed that a positive response on my part would beget a positive response from parents, but I never imagined the response would be so overwhelming! I guess some parents may have had negative experiences when they were in school and hence probably aren't eager to be involved with education. Sharing positive comments about their children helped them to feel accepted. In turn, they were willing to reciprocate."

"I think it takes more than that," replied Ms. White. "If it weren't for a long-lasting relationship with Ms. Chanthala and Mr. Nguyen, our parent involvement programs would have failed. I think the key is to nurture relationships with community leaders."

The bell rang and the teachers left for their next hour of class. On his way back to class, Mr. Jordan wondered which of the ideas he should pursue. Perhaps both, he thought.

Questions for Reflection

1. Do you think that Mr. Randall's story is credible? Why or why not?
2. What are the greatest obstacles that keep parents, and particularly parents who are not part of the dominant culture, from participating in schools?
3. What personal experiences have you had with eliciting parent involvement in a school or classroom? What strategies have worked? What strategies have not worked?
4. What evidence exists to suggest that parent involvement has an impact on a child's academic success?
5. Some parents doubt the value of schooling as a path by which their children might gain access to cultural capital. How would you persuade them of the value of education for their children?

Activity for Extending Thinking

1. Summarize in writing one of the Readings for Extending Thinking at the end of this section, or a related reading on parent or community involvement from your primary course text or another source (e.g., the Internet). Be prepared to share your findings in class.

Case 34

College Student Tutors, Field Research, and Professional Development

A teacher explores new resources for helping students improve in reading and at the same time finds opportunities for her own professional development.

Ms. Nelson was in her third year of teaching in an urban school with more than 60 percent students of color. She was confident about her knowledge of her subject matter areas, her ability to develop thematic curricula, and her skills for developing rapport with students. She was a skilled facilitator of learning and an effective classroom manager.

For the second year in a row, Ms. Nelson had noted a significant increase in the number of students who had difficulty reading. She was disappointed by the increase, for she believed that the ability to read was crucial for students since it could limit or enhance their chances for success in all subject matter areas.

At faculty meetings both this year and last, she had inquired about resources for helping students learn to read and comprehend at higher levels. No one in the school seemed to have the requisite knowledge and skills.

On this day, Dr. Watson, a professor of education from a nearby college, was at the faculty meeting. He had asked for and been given permission by the principal to invite ideas for developing programs of mutual benefit to Ms. Nelson's school and his college. He distributed an interest-assessment survey on which faculty were to suggest such programs. When he talked of the possibility of having a college student pair with a pupil from the school and communicate via E-mail, as well as in person, Ms. Nelson got an idea.

After the meeting Ms. Nelson approached the visitor. "Dr. Watson," she began, "do you have a minute?"

"Why, yes," he replied, extending his hand. "Nice to meet you."

"My name is Ms. Nelson." She told him of her concern about the low reading scores of students and asked if there might be some way

in which the college could help. "One thing I could really use would be reading 'buddies' or tutors for my students."

Dr. Watson brightened. "In fact, I teach a class in which students are to develop skills and strategies for helping students become better readers. I would love to develop a clinical experience for them in which they could work with the kinds of students that they will one day teach."

He continued, "I have 20 students per term, and it would be reasonable to require one hour of reading tutoring per week for 10 weeks. They could meet some weeks at your school, and other weeks on our college campus. How would that work for you?"

"That would be wonderful!" replied Ms. Nelson. "In fact," she said, "we could give the students a measure of their reading ability before the tutoring program and again after it to see what effects, if any, it had. I'm sure others on the faculty, as well as Ms. Arndt, our principal, would love to know. If the results are significant, the program could be expanded."

Dr. Watson nodded. "I think that's an excellent idea!"

"Could we meet and discuss this matter further?" asked Ms. Nelson.

"I'd be delighted," said Dr. Watson. "I'll call you tomorrow. What time is best?"

Ms. Nelson identified her preparation period and wrote down her phone number. "I look forward to your call!" she said.

As she headed back toward her room, she thought to herself that developing a new, low-cost program to help students become better readers was a dream come true. And conducting action research in her classroom and making the results known to colleagues were frosting on the cake!

Questions for Reflection

1. Although Ms. Nelson's newfound resource might have potential, a number of issues must be worked out. List the most important issues and how you would address each.

Issue	Method of Addressing
a.	a.
b.	b.

2. What suggestions other than a tutoring program at a college might you make to help Ms. Nelson's students improve their reading? List other school and community resources.
3. Ms. Nelson saw an opportunity to help her students, while learning and growing professionally as she conducted research and took a leadership role in program development in the school.

What other examples of conducting research or taking such a leadership role have you observed?

4. What are your goals for professional development? What resources will be required for you to attain those goals? What are the next steps in the process of goal attainment?

Activities for Extending Thinking

1. In the school in which you have a clinical assignment, or in which you work, attend a staff development workshop or participate in a staff development project being conducted by a practicing teacher. Summarize your insights and be prepared to share in class.
2. Read at least one of the readings listed at the end of this section. Outline the major ideas and give your personal reaction to each.

Design Your Own Case

Parent and Community Involvement

Design a case that would help classmates explore issues related to parent and community involvement. The story can focus on a method or strategy related to a single subject matter area (e.g., English or social studies) or on a more generic method or strategy pertinent to a wider range of subject matter areas. Your issue might also relate to:

- Planning and preparation
- Classroom environment
- Instruction
- Teacher responsibilities*

In selecting a topic, reflect on recent or current field experiences, personal experiences as a student, or accounts of real classroom incidents. Include some demographic data that tell a bit about the community, school, classroom, teacher, students, and curriculum. Include at least one problem for which there is no obvious solution. Use fictitious names of persons and schools to maintain confidentiality. Your case should be approximately two pages in length (typed, double-spaced) and should include three to four Questions for Reflection, and one or two Activities for Extending Thinking. Following is a form entitled "Design Your Own Case." It outlines categories for developing your case, as well as for developing criteria for assessing responses to your Questions for Reflection and your Activities for Extending Thinking.

*The four categories are from Danielson, C. (1996). *Enhancing professional practice: A framework for teaching.* Alexandria, VA: Association for Supervision and Curriculum Development.

Design Your Own Case

Author Name(s): ____________________

Title of Case: ____________________ **Grade Level(s):** ________

Subject Matter Area (e.g., science): ____________________

Generic Teaching Topic (e.g., planning, grading): ____________________

Contextual Information:

____

Community Factors:

____

School Factors:

____

Classroom Factors:

____

Teacher Characteristics:

____

Student Characteristics:

____

Characteristics of Curriculum:

____

Story: ____________________

____

____

____

____

Questions for Reflection:

1. ____________________

____

2. ____________________

____

3. ____________________

____

Activities for Extending Thinking:

1. ____

____

2. ____

____

Criteria for assessing responses to your Questions for Reflection:

List criteria (e.g., response is clear, consistent with research or best practice, generalized to an appropriate degree—not overgeneralized, valid—based on facts in the case, relevant to an issue in the case, other).

1. ____

____

2. ____

____

Responses to Questions for Reflection:

List what you would consider to be examples of acceptable and unacceptable responses.

	Acceptable	Unacceptable
1. a.	____________	____________
b.	____________	____________
2. a.	____________	____________
b.	____________	____________
3. a.	____________	____________
b.	____________	____________

Responses to Activities for Extending Thinking:

List examples of acceptable and unacceptable responses.

1.	____________	____________
2.	____________	____________

 READINGS FOR EXTENDING THINKING 

Burron, A. (1995). Heed community values if you value reform. *Educational Leadership, 53*(2), 92–93.

Clark, C. S. (1995). Parents and schools. *CQ-Researcher, 5*(3), 51–69.

Dornbusch, S. M., & Glasgow, K. L. (1996). The structural context of family-school relations. In A. Booth & J. F. Dunn (Eds.), *Family-school links: How do they affect educational outcomes?* (pp. 35–44). Mahwah, NJ: Lawrence Erlbaum.

Evans, I. M., Okifuji, A., & Thomas, A. D. (1995). Home-school partnerships: Involving families in the educational process. In I. M. Evans, T. Chicchelli, M. Cohen, & N. P. Schaperv (Eds.), *Staying in school: Partnerships for educational change* (pp. 23–40). Baltimore, MD: Paul H. Brookes.

Finders, M., & Lewis, C. (1994). Why parents don't come to school. *Educational Leadership, 51*(8), 50–54.

Hidalgo, N. M., Bright, J. A., San-Fong, S., Swap, S. M., & Epstein, J. L. (1995). Research on families, schools, and communities: A multicultural perspective. In J. A. Banks & C. A. M. Banks (Eds.), *Handbook of research on multicultural education* (pp. 498–524). New York: Macmillan.

Hildebrand, V., Phenice, L., Gray, M., & Hines, R. (1996). *Knowing and serving diverse families.* Upper Saddle River, NJ: Merrill/Prentice Hall.

Manning, M. L. (1995). Understanding culturally diverse parents and families. *Equity and Excellence in Education, 28*(1), 52–57.

Morrow, R. D. (1991). The challenges of Southeast Asian parental involvement. *Principal, 70*(3), 20–22.

Spaulding, S. (1994). 4 steps to effective parent conferences. *Learning, 23*(2), 36.

Steller, A. (1995). Consensus isn't easy. *Educational Leadership, 53*(2), 94–95.

Studer, J. R. (1993/1994). Listen so that parents will speak. *Childhood Education, 70,* 74–76.

Yoa, E. L. (1988). Working effectively with Asian immigrant parents. *Phi Delta Kappan, 70*(3), 223–225.

Wilson, A. B. (1989, Summer). Theory into practice: An effective program for urban youth. *Educational Horizons,* 136–144.

Internet Sites for Extending Thinking

http: //www.webcrawler.com Type "parent involvement schools" in the "Search" box and click on "Search." Links to sources of handbooks, manuals, and services.

PART 11

TECHNOLOGY AND MULTICULTURALISM

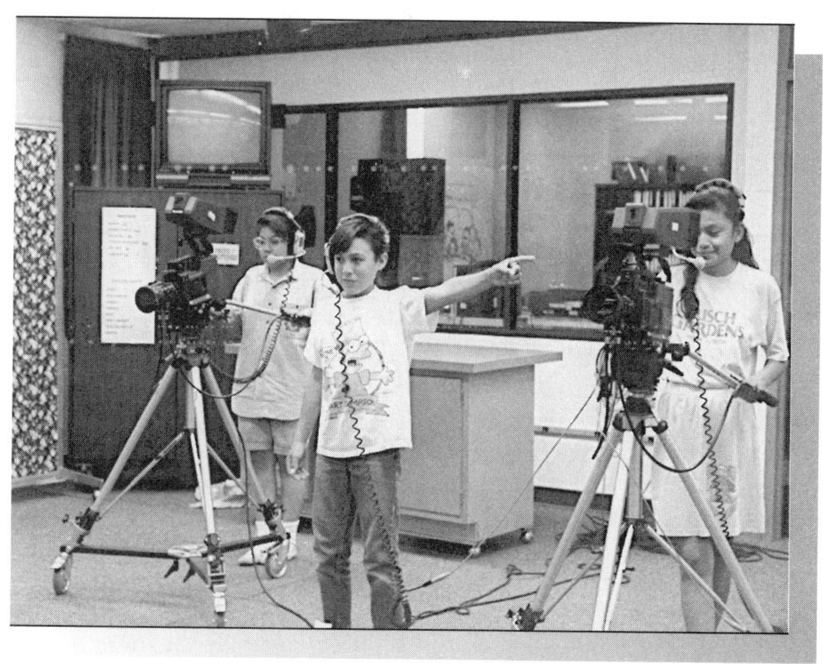

Case 35

Computers and Culturally Diverse Learners

A teacher considers ways in which she can integrate computer technologies and cultural and individual preferences to more effectively meet the socioemotional and academic needs of her students.

Ms. Wright was pleased that for each of the past five years, the school had significantly increased the number of computers and software programs available to students. She believed, however, that neither computers nor software were culturally neutral, that they reflect the assumptions, expectations, and learning styles of their creators (usually white and male), and so she constantly looked for ways to integrate computer culture with the culture of individual students and the culture of the classroom.

To improve cross-cultural skills and intercultural understandings, Ms. Wright had developed an ongoing activity in which each of her students identified and communicated with a pen pal from another country. She was pleased that her classes were enthusiastic about using telecommunications technology to learn about the beliefs, behaviors, and values of persons of other cultures.

In activities involving research on the Internet, Ms. Wright encouraged multidirectional learning. She was as eager to learn from students as she was to have them learn from her. In addition, she encouraged students to help one another whenever possible.

Ms. Wright made every attempt to use computer technology to support a variety of individual and cultural differences. For example, she used visual and graphic representations preferred by some Native American students as a way of understanding; she established pairs and trios at computers as a way to meet the preference for cooperative learning of many black, Asian, and Hispanic students; and she provided an overview and review of material, thereby adding a more global, less fragmented view preferred by many of her culturally diverse students. In each of her classes, Ms. Wright had several limited English-proficiency (LEP) students of Russian, Croatian, and Puerto Rican heritage. While her LEP students had demonstrated re-

markable adaptability, their limited English proficiency kept them a bit behind the other students in learning course content. To accommodate her LEP students' need to learn English, Ms. Wright would often allocate the last 15 minutes of class for the LEP students to complete computer drill-and-practice programs on English grammar, usage, and punctuation. During this same time, non-LEP students would engage in enrichment computer programs requiring creative problem solving in the course content. Ms. Wright believed that this was the best way to attend to the particular needs of both groups of students. By the fifth week of the term, Juan and Vicki, two of her LEP students, had politely reported that the grammar and usage worksheets on the computer were "boring." "We are learning some English, I guess," said Juan, "But, I get tired of doing the same thing almost every day."

Ms. Wright replied, "I think that using technology to help me meet the differing needs of two groups of students is effective and efficient. This way I'm able to help you as well as the other students."

Juan and Vicki appeared unconvinced.

Questions for Reflection

1. What do you consider to be the strengths of Ms. Wright's attempts to use a variety of software programs to address the different learning styles of her diverse student body?
2. What would you change about her approach?
3. Identify other cultural differences in styles of learning. How can educational computing technologies help address these cultural differences in learning?
4. Assess Ms. Wright's role in teaching English to her LEP students. Should she change her role? If so, how?
5. What biases might be inherent in computer and related technologies? How would you adapt your approach to using computer technologies so as to eliminate such biases?
6. What other issues must teachers confront in order to achieve technology equity in their classrooms? For each issue identified, suggest a promising strategy, technique, or approach for addressing the issue.

Activities for Extending Thinking

1. Discuss with female students and students of color their assessment of the degree to which software on the Internet, on disk,

and on CD-ROM is bias free and compatible with their styles of learning. Summarize key findings in writing.

2. Design a classroom activity in which students question software developers (programmers and designers) about the degree to which their products address cultural differences in users. Summarize your findings in writing.

Case 36

Inaccessibility of Web Sites to Students Who Are Blind

A student who is blind finds it impossible to access Web sites designed to take advantage of the graphic capabilities of browsers.

Amanda was a bright, creative, and cooperative student. Blind from birth, she had faced and overcome the many physical, intellectual, and social challenges she encountered. Usually optimistic, she could, like sighted students, have days when she felt like a victim of circumstance. Today was one of those days.

Mr. Grant, Amanda's social studies teacher, had taken the class to the computer lab to give them the opportunity to locate Internet resources for their assigned projects. When Amanda raised her hand for help, Mr. Grant responded.

"Yes, Amanda? May I help you?" he asked.

"I'm having trouble with some of the Web sites. The ones with text are accessible—my computer can read the responses aloud. However, those with graphical Web browsers are inaccessible—my computer can't report pictures. I get lost!" she said with frustration in her voice.

"I understand," replied Mr. Grant. "Tai is working on a related topic, and in fact, she has collected nearly all the citations that she will need for her project. I'll ask her to help you, if that's okay with you."

"That's cool," said Amanda. "We get along well, and I'm sure it won't take long. I already have several text-based sites that I can use."

"You may want to start with the Web page 'Bobby.' As you know, it will display the page and highlight the features that would be difficult or impossible for a person who is visually disabled to use," added Mr. Grant.

"I will. I've used it before. Thanks for your help," said Amanda appreciatively.

Tai accepted Mr. Grant's request that she help Amanda. She was proud to have been selected to play the role of teacher.

Questions for Reflection

1. Assess Mr. Grant's response to Amanda's problem. How, if at all, would you change it?
2. What other technological challenges exist for students with special needs? (For example, in the future, people who are deaf may have trouble using full-motion video transmission over the Internet unless text captions are included on the screen along with the images.)
3. Design a social-action activity through which your students attempt to rectify a technology-based injustice toward students with special needs. (For example, communicate with the World Wide Web Consortium [www.w3.org] in Cambridge or directly with designers to ensure that standards are in place to protect persons with special needs.)

Activities for Extending Thinking

1. Select a resource from the Readings for Extending Thinking list at the end of this section or from another source, such as your primary text. Summarize key insights related to the use of technology with special-needs students.
2. Interview a special-education resource teacher or a computer resource teacher regarding programs he or she would recommend for the special-needs students you teach (or will teach). List at least three recommended programs and cite their strengths, weaknesses, and how they relate to general course goals.
3. Interview a teacher in your licensure area about ways in which, using computers, he or she accommodates students at varying levels of knowledge and skill. List several guidelines that you could recommend to your classmates. Summarize your findings in writing (one to two pages).

 Design Your Own Case 

Technology and Multiculturalism

Design a case that would help classmates explore issues related to technology and multiculturalism. The story can focus on a method or strategy related to a single subject matter area (e.g., English or social studies) or on a more generic method or strategy pertinent to a wider range of subject matter areas. Your issue might also relate to:

- Planning and preparation
- Classroom environment
- Instruction
- Teacher responsibilities*

In selecting a topic, reflect on recent or current field experiences, personal experiences as a student, or accounts of real classroom incidents. Include some demographic data that tell a bit about the community, school, classroom, teacher, students, and curriculum. Include at least one problem for which there is no obvious solution. Use fictitious names of persons and schools to maintain confidentiality. Your case should be approximately two pages in length (typed, double-spaced) and should include three to four Questions for Reflection, and one or two Activities for Extending Thinking. Following is a form entitled "Design Your Own Case." It outlines categories for developing your case, as well as for developing criteria for assessing responses to your Questions for Reflection and your Activities for Extending Thinking.

*The four categories are from Danielson, C. (1996). *Enhancing professional practice: A framework for teaching.* Alexandria, VA: Association for Supervision and Curriculum Development.

DESIGN YOUR OWN CASE

Author Name(s): ______________________________

Title of Case: ______________________ **Grade Level(s):** ________

Subject Matter Area (e.g., science): ______________________

Generic Teaching Topic (e.g., planning, grading): ________________

Contextual Information:

____

Community Factors:

____

School Factors:

____

Classroom Factors:

____

Teacher Characteristics:

____

Student Characteristics:

____

Characteristics of Curriculum:

____

Story: ______________________________

____

____

____

____

Questions for Reflection:

1. ______________________________

____

2. ______________________________

____

3. ______________________________

____

Activities for Extending Thinking:

1. ____

____

2. ____

____

Criteria for assessing responses to your Questions for Reflection:

List criteria (e.g., response is clear, consistent with research or best practice, generalized to an appropriate degree—not overgeneralized, valid—based on facts in the case, relevant to an issue in the case, other).

1. ____

____

2. ____

____

Responses to Questions for Reflection:

List what you would consider to be examples of acceptable and unacceptable responses.

	Acceptable	Unacceptable
1. a.	____________	____________
b.	____________	____________
2. a.	____________	____________
b.	____________	____________
3. a.	____________	____________
b.	____________	____________

Responses to Activities for Extending Thinking:

List examples of acceptable and unacceptable responses.

1.	____________	____________
2.	____________	____________

Readings for Extending Thinking

Arnove, R. F. (1999). Reframing comparative education:The dialectic of the global and the local. In R. F. Arnove & C.A.Torres (Eds.), *Comparative education:The dialectic of the global and the local* (pp. 1-23). New York: Rowman & Littlefield.

Banks, J. A. (2001). *Cultural diversity and education: Foundations, curriculum and teaching* (4th ed.). Boston:Allyn & Bacon.

Brodkin, K. (1998). *How Jews became White folks and what that says about race in America.* New Brunswick, NJ: Rutgers University Press.

Chisholm, I. M. (1994). Culture and technology: Implications for multicultural teacher education. *Journal of Information Technology and Teacher Education, 3*(2), 213-228.

Cochran-Smith, M. (2000). Blind vision: Unlearning racism in teacher education. *Harvard Educational Review, 72*(2), 157-190.

Cummins, J. (1997). *Brave new schools: Challenging cultural illiteracy through global learning networks.* New York: St. Martin's Press.

Fang, F. (1996, November). Traveling the Internet in Chinese. *Educational Leadership,* 27-29.

Guggenheim, C. (1995). *The shadow of hate:A history of intolerance in America* [videotape]. Available from Teaching Tolerance, 400 Washington Avenue, Montgomery, AL 36104.

Howard, G. (1999). *We can't teach what we don't know:White teachers, multiracial schools.* New York:Teachers College Press.

International Society for Technology and Education. (1993). *Curriculum guidelines for accreditation of educational computing and technology programs.* Eugene, OR:Author.

Jacobson, M. F. (1998). *Whiteness of a different color: European immigrants and the alchemy of race.* Cambridge, MA: Harvard University Press.

Jordahl, G. (1995, January). Bringing schools closer with "distance" learning. *Technology and Learning, 15*(4), 16-19.

Keyes, G. K. (1994, Fall). Motivating reluctant students. *Teaching Exceptional Children,* 20-23.

Ladson-Billings, G. (1999). Preparing teachers for diversity: Historical perspectives, current trends, and future directions. In L. Darling-Hammond & G. Sykes (Eds.), *Teaching as the learning profession* (pp. 86-123). San Francisco: Jossey-Bass.

McDonald, J., Lynch, W., & Kearsley, G. (1996, July). Unfilled promises: Can technology help close the equity gap? Maybe—but it hasn't happened yet. *The American School Board Journal,* 26-28.

McIntosh, P. (1997). White privilege: Unpacking the invisible knapsack. In V. Cyrus (Ed.), *Experiencing race, class, and gender* (2nd ed., pp. 194-198). Mountain View, CA: Mayfield.

Meagher, M. (1995, October). Learning English on the Internet. *Educational Leadership,* 88–90.

Nicaise, M., & Barnes, D. (1996, May/June). The union of technology, constructivism, and teacher education. *Journal of Teacher Education, 47*(3), 205–212.

Nieto, S. (1999). *The light in their eyes: Creating multicultural learning communities.* New York: Teachers College Press.

Northrup, P. T., & Little, W. (1996, May/June). Establishing instructional technology benchmarks for teacher preparation programs. *Journal of Teacher Education, 47*(3), 213–222.

Pacino, M.A., & Pacino, J. L. (1996, January). Multimedia and cultural diversity. *T.H.E. Journal,* 70–71.

Pool, T. S., Blanchard, S. M., & Hale, S.A. (1995, January/February). From over the Internet: Users discuss a new direction for learning. *TechTrends,* pp. 24–28.

Rosenstein, J. (Writer, Producer, Ed.). (1997). *In whose honor? American Indian mascots in sports* [videotape]. Available from New Day Films, 22D Hollywood Avenue, Hohokus, NJ 07423, 888-367-9154.

Ross, P. (1995, February). Relevant telecomputing activities. *The Computing Teacher, 22*(5), 28–30.

Ryba, K., Selby, L., & Nolan, P. (1995, October). Computers empower students with special needs. *Educational Leadership,* 83–84.

Schofield, J. W. (2001). The colorblind perspective in school: Causes and consequences. In J.A. Banks & C.A.M. Banks (Eds.), *Multicultural education: Issues and perspectives* (4th ed., pp. 327–352). New York: John Wiley.

U.S. Congress, Office of Technology Assessment. (1995). *Teachers and technology: Marking the connection.* Washington, DC: U.S. Government Printing Office.

Internet Sites for Extending Thinking

http://www.webcrawler.com Type "technology multiculturalism schools" in the "Search" area and click on "Search."

http://www.looksmart.com Type "teaching and learning with technology course" in the "Search the Web" area and click on "Search."

You will find: featured listings, (e.g., technology course descriptions); directory categories, (e.g., information on technology training courses and programs); reviewed Web sites, (e.g., texts on computer usage in teaching); guides to teaching with the web; and other services, (e.g., job search guides).

APPENDIX A

Creating Additional Context for a Given Case

Each case in this text is sufficiently complex to allow for multiple levels of analysis and multiple interpretations. Even so, it is important to bring your own knowledge and personal purpose to the analysis of a given case. Hence, the context of each case has not been highly prescribed. For example, many of the cases do not indicate grade level, thereby allowing for a variety of readers to bring their own grade-level context to the case.

Therefore, as suggested in the introduction, prior to analyzing a given case, you are invited to modify its context. Your instructor will help decide which cases might be modified and the extent of the modifications and will direct you to do so individually, in small groups, or as a class.

When so directed by your instructor, include factors that make the case richer, more authentic, or more personally meaningful to you, your small group, or your class. You may want to re-create a context that resembles a school in which you are currently completing a field experience or in which you are teaching, or you may want to create a setting representing the type of school that you hope to work in some day. Include one or two factors from the following categories.

Characteristics of the community. You might include such factors as proportion of socioeconomic, ethnic, and religious groups and the sociopolitical attitudes of various community groups.

Characteristics of the school. You might include demographics related to the ethnic, religious, and special needs make-up of the student body; curricular and extracurricular emphases of the school; and recent school reform efforts.

Nature of the characters and the classroom. You might include information such as personal characteristics (e.g., physical appearance, social abilities, mannerisms and behavioral habits, intellectual abilities, and teaching or learning styles) or grade level of the class, physical arrangement of the classroom, type of curriculum, and daily schedule of the classes.

In summary, prior to analyzing each case assigned by your instructor, take a few minutes to list two or three additional contextual variables that you believe are important.

Possible Cultural Contexts

Each of the cases will generate a richer and more meaningful discussion if set in an authentic educational and cultural context. To that end, several options are possible:

Scenario 1. Decide that the school and classroom in which the case takes place are very diverse—with proportions of students of color, lower socioeconomic status, disability, and the like *greater than those of the general population.* (See Tables 1.1 and 1.2 for estimated populations of minority groups in the United States.)

Scenario 2. Specify that the diversity in the community, school, and classroom in which the case takes place is *equal to that of the general population.*

Scenario 3. Specify that the diversity in the case school is equal to that of the school in which you are completing or have completed a field experience. It is recommended that this option be selected only when a specific and significant need suggests it. For example, if a school in which you work as a teacher's aide, a student teacher, or a teacher is 98 percent white and has recently experienced racial tension, you might decide to add such issues to a given case.

In addition to the types of diversity outlined in the tables, students in schools vary in other ways, including language, religious affiliation, and national creed. The reader is referred to other multicultural education sources for statistics on other groups and for additional data on the groups cited earlier.

Based on the percentages of various groups in the United States as listed in Tables 1.1 and 1.2, the composition of a "typical" classroom of 30* students would be as shown in Table 1.3:

Table 1.1 Estimated Population of Ethnic Groups in the United States, According to Race, Hispanic Origin, and Jewish and Muslim Origins, 1990

Race	*Percentage*
All Persons	***100.0***
White Americans	80.3
African-Americans	12.1

*Because a given student may well belong to more than one group, the total number of students listed exceeds 30.

Table 1.1 (Continued)

American Indian, Eskimo, or Aleut	0.8
American Indians	0.8
Aleuts	0.0
Asian or Pacific Islander	2.9
Chinese Americans	0.7
Japanese Americans	0.3
Asian Indian	0.3
Korean Americans	0.3
Vietnamese	0.2
Native Hawaiians	0.1
Samoans	0.0
Guamanians	0.0
Other Asian or Pacific Islander	0.3
Other	3.9
Hispanic Origin	
All Persons	***100.0***
Hispanic Origin	9.0
Mexican	5.4
Puerto Rican	1.1
Cuban	0.4
Other Hispanic	2.0
Not of Hispanic Origin	91.0
Jewish and Muslim Origin	
All Persons	***100.0***
Jewish	2.8
Muslim	2.1

Source: Bennett, C. L. *Comprehensive Multicultural Education:Theory and Practice* (3rd ed.). Copyright (c)1995 by Allyn & Bacon. Reprinted/adapted by permission.

Table 1.2 Estimated Percentage of Children in Poverty, with Disabilities, and of Gay/Lesbian/Bisexual Orientation

Poverty	***Percentage***
Children under age of 18 who are poor (Reed & Sautter, 1990)	20
Exceptionality	
Children identified as disabled for purposes of special education services (U.S. Department of Education, 1994)	7.4
Affectional orientation	
Persons of gay/lesbian/bisexual orientation (Kalota et al., 1994)	10

Table 1.3 Composition of a Classroom of 30 Students*

Students	*Number*
White	24
African-American	4
Asian	1
American Indian	1
Hispanic	3
Jewish	1
Muslim	1
Poor	6
Disabled	2–3
Gay/lesbian/bisexual	3

*Based on estimated population of ethnic, socioeconomic class, poverty, exceptionality, and affectional orientation

Obviously, such a "typical" class rarely exists. It is constructed here for those who would want to set the cases provided in a classroom representing the diversity of persons in the general population. Because the student bodies in many schools consist of much greater proportions of ethnic diversity than does the general population, when analyzing a given case, you should assume that the story takes place in such a school. Doing so will better prepare you for a career that might well include teaching in a school with a rich diversity of students.

Once you have predetermined the ethnic, socioeconomic, religious, exceptionality, and affectional orientation of the students in a case, establish other classroom, school, and community characteristics that will further provide the context for the case. For example, specify factors such as the following:

- Number of students served in the school
- Number of students in the particular classroom
- School budget
- Performance levels of students on statewide achievement tests

Furthermore, specify the following:

- Whether the school tracks students into several levels
- Whether the school has access to tutors and student teachers in a teacher education program in a local college
- Whether the school has class periods of a certain length (e.g., 50, 60, or 90 minutes)

- Whether the school has stand-alone and online access to sophisticated computer and related technologies
- Whether the school has a well-developed parent-involvement program

Examples of contexts that might be designed as a basis for the analysis of a given case follow.

Example I. Longfellow School serves 1,000 low- and low-middle-income students living in the inner city. Typical classroom size is 25 students. The student body is 40 percent African-American, 10 percent Hispanic-American, 5 percent Asian-American, 5 percent Native American, and 40 percent white. Approximately 20 percent of these students are Jewish. Student scores on standardized achievement tests are in the 70th percentile. The school divides students into three tracks. Thirty-nine percent of graduates go on to college. Reform efforts have moved the school to the fore in terms of offering a well-developed multicultural curriculum.

Example II. Lincoln School in a city of 40,000 serves 500 low-SES pupils. The student body is 70 percent white, 20 percent Native American, and 10 percent African-American. Approximately 40 percent of the students come from farms. Fifty percent of pupils come from single-parent families, and half are from families that claim to be devoutly Catholic. Class size in Lincoln is 30 students per room. Each room has two computers with Internet interface, and two computer labs of 20 computers each are available to teachers. Except for the progressive approach to technology, the curriculum is relatively traditional. Parent involvement in school activities is low. Each of these examples emphasizes different characteristics in terms of ethnicity, SES, religion, family structure, curriculum, and the like. Each could have been more or less elaborate, depending on the nature of the case to be analyzed, the needs and interests of the students analyzing the case, and the goals of the course or workshop within which the case is used.

APPENDIX B

Banks's Approaches for the Integration of Multicultural Content*

Approach	*Description*	*Examples*	*Strengths*	*Problems*
Contributions	Heros, cultural components, holidays, and other discrete elements related to ethnic groups are added to the curriculum on special days, occasions, and celebrations.	Famous Mexican Americans are studied only during the week of Cinco de Mayo (May 5). African Americans are studied during African-American History Month in February but rarely during the rest of the year. Ethnic foods are studied in the first grade with little attention devoted to the cultures in which the foods are embedded.	Provides a quick and relatively easy way to put ethnic content into the curriculum. Gives ethnic heroes visibility in the curriculum alongside mainstream heroes. Is a popular approach among teachers and educators.	Results in a superficial understanding of ethnic cultures. Focuses on the lifestyles and artifacts of ethnic groups and reinforces sterotypes and misconceptions. Mainstream criteria are used to select heroes and cultural elements for inclusion in the curriculum.
Additive	This approach consists of the addition of content, concepts, themes, and perspectives to the curriculum without changing its structures.	Adding the book *The Color Purple* to a literature unit without reconceptualizing the unity or giving the students the background knowledge to understand the book. Adding a unit on the Japanese-American internment to a U.S. history course without treating the Japanese in any other unit. Leaving the core curriculum intact but adding an ethnic studies course as an elective that focuses on a specific ethnic group.	Makes it possible to add ethnic content to the curriculum without changing its structure, which requires substantial curriculum changes and staff development. Can be implemented within the existing curriculum structure.	Reinforces the idea that ethnic history and culture are not integral parts of U.S. mainstream culture. Students view ethnic groups from Anglocentric and Eurocentric perspectives. Fails to help students understand how the dominant culture and ethnic cultures are interconnected and interrelated.

*Banks, J. A. (1997). Approaches to cultural curriculum reform. In Banks, J. A. & Banks, C.A.M. (Eds.), *Multicultural education: Issues and perspectives* (pp. 229–250). Boston: Allyn & Bacon . Reprinted by permission of John Wiley & Sons, Inc.

Approach	***Description***	***Examples***	***Strengths***	***Problems***
Transformation	The basic goals, structure, and nature of the curriculum are changed to enable students to view concepts, events, issues, problems, and themes from the perspectives of diverse cultural, ethnic, and racial groups.	A unit on the American Revolution describes the meaning of the revolution to Anglo revolutionaries, Anglo loyalists, African-Americans, Indians, and the British. A unit on 20th-century U.S. literature includes works by William Faulkner, Joyce Carol Oates, Langston Hughes, N. Scott Momaday, Saul Bellow, Maxine Hong Kingston, Rudolfo A. Anaya, and Piri Thomas.	Enables students to understand the complex ways in which diverse racial and cultural groups participated in the formation of U.S. society and culture. Helps reduce racial and ethnic encapsulation. Enables diverse ethnic, racial, and religious groups to see their cultures, ethos, and perspectives in the school curriculum. Gives students a balanced view of the nature and development of U.S. culture and society. Helps to empower victimized racial, ethnic, and cultural groups.	The implementation of this approach requires substantial curriculum revision, in-service training, and the identification and development of materials written from the perspectives of various racial and cultural groups. Staff development for the institutionalization of this approach must be continual and ongoing.
Social Action	In this approach, students identify important social problems and issues, gather pertinent data, clarify their values on the issues, make decisions, and take reflective actions to help resolve the issue or problem.	A class studies prejudice and discrimination in its school and decides to take actions to improve race relations in the school. A class studies the treatment of ethnic groups in a local newspaper and writes a letter to the publisher suggesting ways that the treatment of ethnic groups in the newspaper should be improved.	Enables students to improve their thinking, value analysis, decision-making and social-action skills. Enables students to improve their data-gathering skills. Helps students develop a sense of political efficacy. Helps students improve their skills to work in groups.	Requires a considerable amount of curriculum planning and materials identification. May be longer in duration than more traditional teaching units. May focus on problems and issues considered controversial by some members of the school staff and citizens of the community. Students may be able to take few meaningful actions that contribute to the resolution of the social issue or problem.

APPENDIX C

Matrix: Interpersonal Competence Cases, Multicultural Content Cases

The following is a taxonomy that places each of the cases in the casebook into one of the following areas:

- **Interpersonal Competence.** Ability to interpret intentional communications (language, signs, gestures), some unconscious cues (body language), and customs in cultural styles different from one's own. Emphasis is on empathy and interpersonal communication (Bennett, C., *Multicultural Education,* 1999, p. 30). Relates to interaction with students.
- **Multicultural Content.** Knowledge of history, heritage, and culture of persons of cultures different from one's own. Relates to subject matter (curriculum) planned for or delivered to students.

	Interpersonal Competence	Multicultural Content
Part 2 Gender		
Case 1 Reinforcing Specifically	X	
Case 2 Fridays Are Video Days	X	
Case 3 Developing Skills of Critical Analysis: Exposing the Myths of Films and Fairy Tales		X
Case 4 Dwight, What Do You Think?		X
Part 3 Ethnicity		
Case 5 Lets All Make Up the Rules for Our Classroom	X	
Case 6 Other Cultures Celebrate Thanksgiving, Too		X
Case 7 When Will I Ever Use This? Mathematics and Social Justice		X
Case 8 Overlook the Stereotypes— It's Art		X
Case 9 Presidents of Mount Rushmore: Another Perspective		X
Case 10 U.S. Folk Heroes		X
Case 11 Culture and Learning Styles	X	
Case 12 Respect? Let's Talk About It	X	X

	Interpersonal Competence	Multicultural Content
Part 4 Race		
Case 13 The Knowledge Base on Diversity: An Aid for Teachers		X
Case 14 Students Right an Injustice	X	X
Case 15 I'm Glad You're Back	X	
Case 16 Hey, My Niggah: Inclusive and/or Demeaning?	X	
Case 17 Hey, Teach—You Trippin' on Me, but Not on the White Kids!	X	
Part 5 Socioeconomic Status		
Case 18 A New Student and a Lesson in Geography	X	
Case 19 Gangs and the Victims of Violence	X	X
Case 20 How Should I Grade Danielle?	X	
Case 21 Rewarding Respectful Behavior	X	
Part 6 Religion		
Case 22 Isn't the Christmas Tree a Christian Symbol?	X	X
Case 23 My Persuasive Essay Is "Why We Should Follow Jesus"	X	X
Case 24 Planning for Religious Diversity: Special Needs of Muslim Students	X	X
Part 7 Special Needs		
Case 25 We Only Meant It as a Joke	X	
Case 26 Structuring for Success in a Mainstreamed Classroom	X	
Case 27 Anthony, Please Don't Push: Developing an IEP	X	
Part 8 Affectional Orientation		
Case 28 Not in My Group—He's Gay!	X	
Case 29 In Islam, Homosexuality Is a Sin and a Crime	X	X
Part 9 Language		
Case 30 You'll Need Both Black English Vernacular and Standard English	X	X
Case 31 They Speak English and Spanish Well, but a Learning Disability Creates Problems in Reading and Writing	X	
Case 32 A Bilingual Teacher's Aide Assesses His New School	X	X
Part 10 Parent and Community Involvement		
Case 33 It Takes a Village	X	

	Interpersonal Competence	Multicultural Content
Case 34 College Student Tutors, Field Research, and Professional Development	X	
Part 11 Technology and Multiculturalism		
Case 35 Computers and Culturally Diverse Learners	X	
Case 36 Inaccessibility of Web Sites to Students Who Are Blind	X	

BIBLIOGRAPHY

General Education

Anderson, E. M., Redman, G. L., & Rogers, C. (1991). *Self-esteem for tots to teens.* Wayzata, MN: Parenting and Teaching Publications.

Clark, C., & Lampert, M. (1986). The study of teacher thinking: Implications for teacher education. *Journal of Teacher Education, 37*(5), 27–31.

Covington, M. (1984). The self-worth theory of motivation. *The Elementary School Journal, 85*(1), 5–20.

Danielson, C. (1996). *Enhancing professional practice: A framework for teaching.* Alexandria, VA: Association for Supervision and Curriculum Development.

Davis, L. (1996, April). Equality in education: An agenda for urban schools. *Equity & Excellence in Education,* 61–67.

Frey, D., & Carlock, C. J. (1989). *Enhancing self-esteem.* Muncie, IN: Accelerated Development Publishers.

Gage, N. L. (1978). *The scientific basis of the art of teaching.* New York: Perennial Library.

Glasser, W. (1985). *Control theory in the classroom.* New York: Teachers College Press.

Kennedy, M. M. (1991). *An agenda for research on teacher learning.* (Special Report). East Lansing, MI: National Center for Research on Teacher Learning.

Kleinfeld, J. (1992). Learning to think like a teacher: The study of cases. In J. H. Shulman (Ed.), *Case methods in teacher education* (pp. 33–49). New York: Teachers College Press.

Kolata, G., Laumann, E., Michael, R., & Gagnon, J. (1994). *Sex in America.* Chicago: National Opinion Research Center, University of Chicago.

Marzano, R. J. (1992). *A different kind of classroom: Teaching with dimensions of learning.* Alexandria, VA: Association for Supervision and Curriculum Development.

McNergney, R., Herbert, J., & Ford, R. (1994). Cooperation and competition in cases-based education. *Journal of Teacher Education, 45*(5), 339–345.

Merseth, K. K. (1991). *The case for cases in teacher education.* Washington, DC: American Association for Higher Education and the American Association of Colleges for Teacher Education.

Morine-Dershimer, G. (1991). Learning to think like a teacher. *Teaching and Teacher Education,* 7(2), 159–168.

Oja, S., & Sprinthall, N. A. (1978). Psychological and moral development for teachers. In N. A. Sprinthall & R. L. Mosher (Eds.), *Value development as the aim of education* (pp. 117–134). Schenectady, NY: Charter Research Press.

Redman, G. L. (1992). *Building self-esteem in students: A skill and strategy workbook for teachers.* Wayzata, MN: Parenting and Teaching Publications.

Redman, G. L. (1995). *Building self-esteem in children: A skill and strategy workbook for parents.* Wayzata, MN: Parenting and Teaching Publications.

Reed, S., & Sautter, R. (1990). Children of poverty—the status of 12 million young Americans. *Phi Delta Kappan, 71*(10), K1–K12.

Riley, S. S. (1984). *How to generate values in young children: Integrity, honesty, individuality, self-confidence, and wisdom.* Washington, DC: National Association for the Education of Young Children.

Schon, D. A. (1987). *Educating the reflective practitioner.* San Francisco: Jossey-Bass.

Shulman, L. (1992). Toward a pedagogy of cases. In J. H. Shulman, *Case methods in teacher education.* New York: Teachers College Press.

Silverman, R., Welty, W., & Lyon, S. (1994). *Multicultural education cases for teacher problem solving.* New York: McGraw-Hill.

U.S. Department of Education. (1988). Tenth annual report to Congress on the implementation of the handicapped act. Washington, DC: Author.

Sources Containing Case Studies

Cooper, J. M. (1995). *Teacher's problem solving: A casebook of award-winning cases.* Boston: Allyn & Bacon.

Greenword, G. E., & Fillmer, H. T. (1997). *Professional core cases for teacher decision-making.* Upper Saddle River, NJ: Merrill/Prentice Hall.

Hinely, R., & Ford, K. (1995). *Education in Edge City: Cases for reflection and action.* Hillsdale, NJ: Lawrence Erlbaum.

Kaufman, J. M., Mostert, M. P., Nuttycombe, D. G., Trent, S. C., & Hallahan, D. P. (1993). *Managing classroom behavior: A reflective case-based approach.* Boston: Allyn & Bacon.

Kowalski, T. J., Weaver, R. A., & Henson, K. T. (1990). *Case studies on teaching.* New York: Longman.

Shulman, J. H., & Mesa-Bains, A. (Eds.). (1990). *Diversity in the classroom: A casebook for teachers and teacher education.* San Francisco: Research for Better Schools.

Silverman, R., Welty, W. M., & Lyons, S. (1994a). *Classroom assessment cases for teacher problem solving.* New York: McGraw-Hill.

Silverman, R., Welty, W. M., & Lyons, S. (1994b). *Classroom management cases for teacher problem solving.* New York: McGraw-Hill.

Silverman, R., Welty, W. M., & Lyons, S. (1994c). *Educational psychology cases for teacher problem solving.* New York: McGraw-Hill.

Silverman, R., Welty, W. M., & Lyons, S. (1994d). *Multicultural education cases for teacher problem solving.* New York: McGraw-Hill.

Silverman, R., Welty, W. M., & Lyons, S. (1994e). *Primis education series: Case studies for teacher problem solving.* New York: McGraw-Hill.

Silverman, R., Welty, W. M., & Lyons, S. (1996). *Case studies for teacher problem solving.* New York: McGraw-Hill.

Stipek, D. J. (1988). *Motivation to learn.* Englewood Cliffs, NJ: Prentice Hall.

Wasserman, S. (1993). *Getting down to cases: Learning to teach with case studies.* New York: Teachers College Press.

Watson, C. R. (1997). *Middle school case studies.* Upper Saddle River, NJ: Merrill/Prentice Hall.

Reviews: Case Methods

Anderson, L. M., Blumenfeld, P., Pintrich, P. R., Clark, C. M., Marx, R. W., & Peterson, P. (1995). Educational psychology for teachers: Reforming our courses, rethinking our roles. *Educational Psychologist, 30*(3), 143–158.

Harrington, H., & Garrison, M. (1992). Cases as shared inquiry: A dialogical model of teacher preparation. *American Educational Research Journal, 29,* 715–735.

Merseth, K. (1996). Cases and case methods in teacher education. In J. Sikula (Ed.), *Handbook of research on teacher education* (pp. 722–746). New York: Macmillan/Simon & Schuster.

Empirical Studies: Case Methods

Levin, B. B. (1994). Using the case method in teacher education: The role of discussion and experience in teachers' thinking about cases. *Teacher and Teacher Education, 10*(2), 1–17.

Levin, B. B. (1996, April). *Learning from discussion: A comparison of computer-based versus face-to-face case discussions.* Paper presented at the American Educational Research Association Conference, New York.

Lundeberg, M. A. (1993). Case discussions in educational psychology. In V. Wolf (Ed.), *Improving the climate of the college classroom* (pp. 159–164). Madison: University of Wisconsin System Office of Equal Opportunity Programs and Policy Studies.

Lundeberg, M.A., Coballes-Vega, C., Daly, K., Bowman, G., Uhren, P., & Greenberg, D. (1995). Wandering around the world: Building multicultural perspectives through K-12 telecommunications projects. *Journal of Technology and Teacher Education, 3*(4), 301–321.

Lundeberg, M.A., & Fawver, J. E. (1994). Thinking like a teacher: Encouraging cognitive growth in case analysis. *Journal of Teacher Education, 45*(4), 289–297.

Lundeberg, M.A., Matthew, D., & Scheurman, G. (1996, April). Looking twice means seeing more: How knowledge affects case analysis. Paper presented at the American Educational Research Association Conference, New York.

Case Methodology

Clandinin, D. J. (1992). Narrative and story in teacher education. In T. Russell & H. Munby (Eds.), *Teachers and teaching: From classroom to reflection.* Washington, DC: Falmer Press.

Greenwood, G., & Parkay, F. W. (1989). *Case studies for teacher decision making.* New York: Random House.

Grossman, P. L. (1992). Teaching and learning with cases: Unanswered questions. In J. H. Shulman (Ed.), *Case methods in teacher education.* New York: Teachers College Press.

Huntchings, P. (1993). *Using cases to improve college teaching: A guide to more reflective practice.* Washington, DC: American Association for Higher Education.

Kagan, D. M., & Tippins, D. J. (1993). Classroom cases as gauges of professional growth. In M. O'Hair & S. Odell (Eds.), *Teacher education yearbook 1: Diversity and teaching* (pp. 98-110). New York: Harcourt Brace Jovanovich and the Association of Teacher Educators.

Merseth, K. (1991). *The case for cases in teacher education.* Washington, DC: American Association for Higher Education.

Schon, D. A. (1983). *The reflective practitioner: How professions think in action.* New York: Basic Books.

Schon, D.A. (1991). *The reflective turn: Case studies in and on educational practice.* New York: Teachers College Press.

Schulman, J. H. (Ed.). (1992). *Case methods in teacher education.* New York: Teachers College Press.

Shulman, J. H., & Mesa-Bains, A. (Eds.). (1993). *Diversity in the classroom: A casebook for teachers and teacher educators.* Hillsdale, NJ: Research for Better Schools and Lawrence Erlbaum.

Sykes, G., & Bird, T. (1992). Teacher education and the case idea. In G. E. Grant (Ed.), *Review of research in education,* Vol. 18. Washington, DC: American Educational Research Association.

Journal Articles and Papers on Case Methods

Albanese, M., & Mitchell, S. (1993). Problem-based learning: A review of literature on its outcomes and implementation issues. *Academic Medicine, 68,* 52-81.

Carter, K., (1993). The place of story in research on teaching and teacher education. *Educational Researcher, 22*(1), 5-12.

Carter, K., & Gonzalez, L. (1993). Beginning teachers' knowledge of classroom events. *Journal of Teacher Education, 44,* 223-232.

Fourtner, A. W., Fourtner, C. R., & Herreid, C. F. (1994). Bad blood: A study of the Tuskegee syphilis project. *Journal of College Science Teaching, 23,* 277-285.

Harrington, H. L. (1994). Perspectives on cases. *International Journal of Qualitative Studies in Education,* 7(2), 117-133.

Harrington, H. L., & Garrison, J. (1992). Cases as shared inquiry: A dialogical model of teacher preparation. *American Educational Research Journal, 29*(4), 715-735.

Herreid, C. F. (1994). Case studies in science: A novel method of science education. *Journal of College Science Teaching, 23,* 221-229.

Kagan, D. M. (1993, Winter). Contexts for the use of classroom cases. *American Educational Research Journal, 30*(4), 703-723.

Kleinfeld, J. (1990a). *Creating cases on your own.* Fairbanks: Department of Education, Rural College, University of Alaska.

Kleinfeld, J. (1990b). The special virtues of the case method in preparing teachers for minority schools. *Teacher Education Quarterly, 17,*(1), 43-51.

Merseth, K. K., & Lacey, C. A. (1993). Weaving stronger fabric: The pedagogical promise of hypermedia and case methods in teacher education. *Teaching & Teacher Education, 9*(3), 283-299.

Sykes, G., & Bird, T. (1992). Teacher education and the case idea. *Review of Research in Education, 18,* 457-521.

Multiculturalism

Banks, J. A. (1991). A curriculum for empowerment, action, and change. In C. E. Sleeter (Ed.), *Empowerment through multicultural education* (pp. 125–142). Albany: State University of New York Press.

Banks, J. A. (1994a). *An introduction to multicultural education.* Boston: Allyn & Bacon.

Banks, J. A. (1994b). *Multiethnic education.* Boston: Allyn & Bacon.

Banks, J. A. (2001). Approaches to multicultural curriculum reform. In J. A. Banks & C. A. Banks (Eds.), *Multicultural education: Issues and perspectives* (4th ed., pp. 225–246). New York: John Wiley & Sons.

Banks, J. A., & Banks, C. A. M. (Eds.).(1997). *Multicultural education: Issues and perspectives.* Boston: Allyn & Bacon.

Belenky, M. F., Clinchy, B. M., Goldberger, N. R., & Tarule, J. M. (1986). *Women's ways of knowing.* New York: Basic Books.

Chisholm, I. M. (1994). Culture and technology: Implications for multicultural teacher education. *Journal of Information Technology and Teacher Education, 3*(2), 213–228.

Christensen, L. (1994). Unlearning the myths that bind us. In B. Bigelow, L. Christensen, & J. Karp (Eds.), *Rethinking our classrooms: Teaching for equity and justice* (pp. 8–13). Milwaukee, WI: Rethinking Our Schools Ltd.

Darder, A. (1991). *Culture and power in the classroom.* New York: Bergin and Garvey.

Gaff, J. G. (1992). Beyond politics: The educational issues inherent in multicultural education. *Change, 24*(1), 31–35.

Gay, G. (1994). *At the essence of learning: Multicultural education.* West Lafayette, IN: Kappa Delta Pi.

Grant, C. A., & Gomez, M. L. (Eds.). (1996). *Making schooling multicultural: Campus and classroom.* Upper Saddle River, NJ: Merrill/Prentice Hall.

Grant, C. A., & Sleeter, C. E. (1998). *Turning on learning.* Upper Saddle River, NJ: Merrill/Prentice Hall.

Helms, J. (Ed.). (1990). *Black and white racial identity: Theory, research, and practice.* Westport, CT: Praeger.

Jennings, T. (1994). Self in connection as a component of human-rights advocacy. *The Journal of Moral Education, 23*(3), 285–295.

Kosmin, B. A. (1991). Highlights of the CJF 1990 national Jewish population survey. New York: Council of the Jewish Federation, pp. 3–6, 10, 20–22, 25–26. Reprinted in Feagin, J., & Feagin, C. (1993). *Racial and ethnic relations* (4th ed.). Englewood Cliffs, NJ: Prentice Hall.

Levine, A., & Cureton, J. (1992). The quiet revolution: Eleven facts about multiculturalism and the curriculum. *Change, 24*(1), 25–29.

Nieto, S. (1999). *The light in their eyes: Creating multicultural learning communities.* New York: Teachers College Press.

Nieto, S. (2000). *Affirming diversity and the sociopolitical context of multicultural education* (3rd ed.). White Plains, NY: Longman.

Phelan, P., Davidson, A. L., & Yu, H. C. (1993). Students' multiple worlds: Navigating the borders of family, peer and school cultures. In A. L. Davidson & P. Phelan (Eds.), *Renegotiating cultural diversity in American schools* (pp. 52–88). New York: Teachers College Press.

Sleeter, C. E., & McLaren, P. L. (Eds.). (1995). *Multicultural education, critical pedagogy, and the politics of difference.* Albany: State University of New York Press.

Spindler, G., & Spindler, L. (Eds.). (1994). *Pathways to cultural awareness: Cultural therapy with teachers and students.* Thousand Oaks, CA: Sage.

Tatum, B. D. (1992). Talking about race, learning about racism: The application of racial identity development theory in the classroom. *Harvard Education Review, 62*(1) 1–24.

Trudgill, P. (1984). *Sociolinguistics: An introduction to language and society.* New York: Penguin Books.

Understanding Islam and the Muslims. (1989). Washington, DC: The Embassy of Saudi Arabia. Reprinted in Bennett, C. (1995). *Comprehensive multicultural education theory and practice.* Needham Heights, MA: Allyn & Bacon.

Internet Resources

General Educational Resources

Edweb	http://www.edwebproject.org
ERIC	http://ericir.syr.edu (lesson plans, databases, and so on)
Internet Public Library	http://www.ipl.org/ref
Kathy Schrock's Guide	http://www.capecod. net// Schrockguide
U.S. Dept. of Education	http://www.ed.gov/lVlib.

Teaching with Technology

T.H.E. Online	http://www.thejournal.com *(Journal of Technology in Higher Education)*
Teaching with Technology	http://www.uvm.edu/~jmorris
Web 66	http://web66.coled.umn.edu (to set up webservers)

Listservs and Newsgroups

Multicultural Education	E-mail: MULTCED@umddumd.edu Subscribe MULTC-ED first name last name http://www.wmht.org/trail/explor02

Education and Cultural Diversity

Teacher Training and Multiculturalism	http://unesco.uneb.edu/ educ news/multiculturalism http://www.valdosta.peachnet.edu/~whuitt/educ.html#mc